From an original contemporary portrait in the possession of the Author.

FOTHERINGHAY

AND

MARY, QUEEN OF SCOTS.

BEING

AN ACCOUNT, HISTORICAL AND DESCRIPTIVE,
OF FOTHERINGHAY CASTLE,
THE LAST PRISON OF MARY, QUEEN OF SCOTS,
AND THE
SCENE OF HER TRIAL AND EXECUTION.

pseud. of Edward Bradley

BY CUTHBERT BEDE:

With Illustrations by the Author,
And an original contemporary portrait of Mary, Queen of Scots,
now first published.

LONDON:
SIMPKIN, MARSHALL, & Co.
OUNDLE: ALFRED KING.
1886.

"DEAR to the Loves, and to the Graces vowed,
The Queen drew back the wimple that she wore;
And to the throng how touchingly she bowed
That hailed her landing on the Cumbrian shore;
Bright as a Star (that, from a heavy cloud
Of pine-tree foliage poised in air, forth darts,
When a soft summer gale at evening parts
The gloom that did its loveliness enshroud)
She smiled: but Time, the old Saturnian Seer,
Sighed on the wing as her foot pressed the strand,
With step prelusive to a long array
Of woes and degradations hand in hand—
Weeping captivity, and shuddering fear
Stilled by the ensanguined block of Fotheringhay."

Wordsworth's Sonnet to "Mary, Queen of Scots."

WITH A

GRATEFUL ACKNOWLEDGMENT

OF A LITERARY AND ARTISTIC FRIENDSHIP,

EXTENDING OVER THIRTY-FIVE YEARS,

AND MUCH KIND HOSPITALITY,

I SUBSCRIBE THIS BOOK

TO

JOHN MOYER HEATHCOTE, Esq.,

OF CONINGTON CASTLE, HUNTINGDONSHIRE,

A BUILDING SO INTIMATELY CONNECTED WITH

FOTHERINGHAY AND MARY, QUEEN OF SCOTS.

Lenton Vicarage,
Grantham,
November, 1885.

PREFACE.

The chief portion of the contents of this book originally appeared in three numbers of "The Leisure Hour," for November, 1865, illustrated with three views, drawn on the wood, by myself, from my own sketches taken in that year.

After an interval of twenty years, Mr. Alfred King, *of Oundle, thought that a re-publication of my account of Fotheringhay would be of interest to the many visitors to that historical spot; and my friend,* Dr. Macaulay, *Editor of "The Leisure Hour," kindly gave me permission to use both the letterpress and illustrations that had appeared in his Magazine.*

I have, however, very carefully revised and corrected what I then wrote, and have made very considerable additions, in order to make the information as complete and accurate as I was able. Fresh illustrations have also been added from my own sketches.

Further, I have supplemented the descriptive details, by a concise history of the trial and execution of Mary, Queen of Scots, derived from the best authorities.

CUTHBERT BEDE.

CONTENTS.

LIST OF ILLUSTRATIONS.

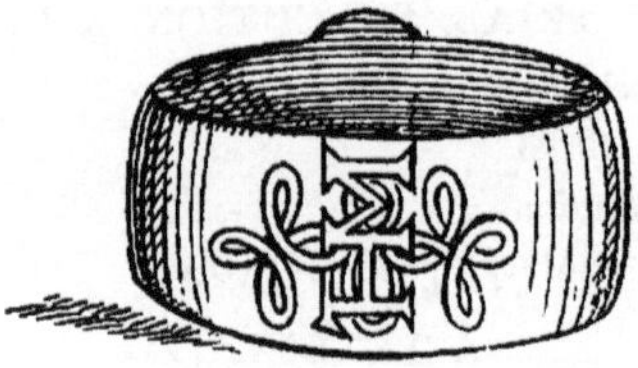

SIGNET-RING OF MARY, QUEEN OF SCOTS.

Found in the ruins of Fotheringhay, and supposed to have been dropped from her finger on the scaffold, and to have been swept away in the bloody sawdust.

FOTHERINGHAY.

CHAPTER I.

Fotheringhay a troubled history.—Its foundation.—Sad Chatillon.—Edward Duke of York.—Proud Cis.—King Edward the Fourth.—Richard the Third.—Catharine of Arragon.—Mary, Queen of Scots.—Queen Elizabeth.

FOTHERINGHAY is a name distinguished in historic annals; but, although from the first its castle was connected with royalty, it would appear in every age to have brought to its princely possessors a heritage of misery and blood. Balliol, York, Plantagenet, and Stuart alike found in Fotheringhay either a troubled home, or a gloomy prison, or the grave of a violent death. Originally built by Mary Stuart's ancestor—that Simon de St. Liz who had married the great niece of William the Conqueror, and who had built a second fortress upon the river Nene at Northampton—the old castle of Fotheringhay had been held by the luckless Balliols; and its last possessor was that Mary of Valence, Countess of

Pembroke, whose husband fell in a tournament upon their bridal day, and whom the poet Gray has celebrated as the

> "Sad Chatillon, on her bridal morn
> That wept her bleeding love."

She passed the long days of her virgin-widowhood at Fotheringhay, devoting herself to the services of religion, and her fortune to the foundation of Pembroke Hall, in the University of Cambridge, to perpetuate the memory of her husband of a few hours.

Her successor in the lordship was Edmund Langley, the fifth son of Edward III, who rebuilt the castle, and left it to his son Edward, Duke of York. He did not, however, live long to enjoy it, for he was slain at the head of his vanguard of English archers in the famous fight of Agincourt, where he was stifled by the heat and by the enemy thronging upon him—for, says the old Chronicle, "being a fatte man, he was smouldered to death." It was his dying wish that he should be buried in the collegiate church of Fotheringhay, which he himself had founded; and there he was accordingly interred on December 1, 1415. The castle then passed to his brother, Richard Plantagenet, Earl of Cambridge, who was beheaded, on suspicion of being in a conspiracy against Henry V. His son, Richard, Duke of York, was the next who held it; and he, too, inherited the Fotheringhay fate, meeting a violent death at the battle of Wakefield Green, together with his second son, Edmund, Earl of Rutland, a lad of twelve, who was barbarously slain in cold blood by Lord Clifford. The bodies of the father and son were removed from Pontefract to Fotheringhay with the greatest pomp, and with a ceremonial of which a full account has been handed down to us, and were buried in the collegiate church on July 22, 1466. Richard's widow, Cecily, Duchess of York—who was the "proud Cis" of the familiar proverb—survived her husband thirty-six years; and, as the "sad Chatillon" had done before her, passed the chief part of her widowhood at Fotheringhay, where also she found her grave.

By the way, Miss Agnes Strickland was slightly in error in fixing the period of the Duchess of York's "sorrowful widowhood" at "thirty years"*—thirty-six is the correct date of widowhood, where, at Fotheringhay, she not only wept away her years, but also saw "the last of her male descendants perish tragically, and the name of Plantagenet become extinct." The pronunciation of her Christian name, together with that of her father, is curiously and phonetically shown by the inscription on the east side of the Communion-table in Fotheringhay Church:—"Sissily, Dutchess of York, Daughter to Raulfe Nevell, first Earl of Westmorland." She and the Dukes of York were first buried in the choir;

* *The Queens of Scotland:* Mary Stuart. Vol. VII, p. 419.

but at the dissolution, when the choir was pulled down by the Duke of Northumberland, their bodies were dug up, and (according to Fuller) lay in the churchyard without any monument until Queen Elizabeth visited Fotheringhay, in 1573, and ordered the bodies to be re-buried in the church, and appropriate monuments to be erected. On opening the coffin of the Duchess Cecily there was found about her neck a silver ribbon with a pardon from Rome, penned in a very fine Roman hand, as fair and fresh to be read as if it had been written yesterday. Such was the account given by Mr. Creuso, a gentleman who dwelt in the college at the same time, to Henry Peacham, who mentions it in his "Complete Gentleman" (p 160).

King Edward the Fourth—son of the Duchess Cecily—occasionally fixed his residence at Fotheringhay, coming there on one occasion by water from Croyland to join his Queen, and, on another occasion, granting an audience here to Alexander, who entered into a covenant to do fealty and homage for the realm of Scotland within six months after he had obtained possession of the crown. During her widowed residence at Fotheringhay, the Duchess Cecily not only had to mourn the tragical fate of her little grandsons, Edward V and his brother, but also to have her grief made more poignant by the thought that their murderer was her own son, who had been born within the walls of Fotheringhay; that Duke of Gloucester who, as King Richard III, was the last of the Plantagenets, and who, having waded to the throne through blood, quitted it by a violent end, yet not before he had accused his mother of the grossest profligacy. Shakespeare, therefore, in his play of "Richard III," makes the duchess say of him, "He is my son, ay, and therein my shame;" and again,

> "And I for comfort have but one false gloss
> That grieves me when I see my shame in him."

And the Shakespearian reader will also call to mind that scene where, in such terrible colours, she depicts her son's character from his very birth at Fotheringhay; where his infancy was "tetchy and wayward"; and then solemnly curses him with this prophetic malediction:—

> "Bloody thou art, bloody will be thy end:
> Shame serves thy life, and doth thy death attend."

Such was the king of England who was born in Fotheringhay Castle, and from whose mother Mary, Queen of Scots was fourth in descent.

After the death of Duchess Cecily, in 1495, the castle was given by Henry VII to his Queen Elizabeth, who was the sole representative of the House of York. Henry VIII settled it in dower upon his unfortunate Queen Catharine of Arragon, who repaired it at great cost, and would seem to have been attached to it, until her royal husband wished to turn it into her prison, when she declared that "to Fotheringhay she would not go, unless bound with cart-ropes and carried thither." But in Mary's reign Fotheringhay really became a state-prison, when Edward Courtney, Earl of Devonshire, was removed thither from the Tower, on a charge of having been implicated in Sir Thomas Wyatt's conspiracy.

Such was the previous history of Fotheringhay Castle up to the period of that terrible tragedy—the imprisonment and execution of Mary, Queen of Scots, which has, as it were, swallowed up the memory of all that had gone before, and caused the name of Fotheringhay to be associated with, and dedicated to, a recollection of the most touching royal death-scene in our country's annals. Into the details of that scene it is not here my province to enter, though they will be narrated at the end of this book. We have to do now with the prison, and not its prisoner; with the past and present of Fotheringhay itself, and not with the doom of its most illustrious and beautiful captive. She who, as Wordsworth has sung, "Dear to the loves, and to the graces vowed," landed on the Cumbrian shore,

"With step prelusive to a long array
Of woes and degradations hand in hand—
Weeping captivity and shuddering fear,
Stilled by the ensanguined block of Fotheringhay"

—though the poet is scarcely correct as to "the shuddering fear." It may have dwelt in the guilty bosom of Elizabeth, but was certainly not shown by Mary, even in the supreme moment of her fate. Yet, if the verse of the poet is faulty, there is a verse in a certain Book which, could a voice have gone up from the banquet-hall of Fotheringhay, might have thus denounced the English queen: "Thou hast consulted shame to thyself by cutting off many people, and hast sinned against thy soul. For the stone shall cry out of the wall, and the beam out of the timber shall answer it."

> "Lo! on that mound, in days of feudal pride,
> Thy towering castle frown'd above the tide;
> Flung wide her gates, where troops of vassals met
> With awe the brow of proud Plantagenet.
>
> "But ah! what chiefs in sable crests appear?
> What bright achievement marks yon warrior's bier?
> 'Tis York's!—From Agincourt's victorious plain,
> They bear the fallen hero o'er the main;
> Through all the land his blooming laurels spread,
> And to thy bosom give the mighty dead.
>
> "When from thy lap the ruthless Richard sprung,
> A boding sound through all thy borders rung:
> It spoke a tale of blood—fair Neville's woe,
> York's murderous hand, and Edward's future foe."*

The history of Fotheringhay would seem to have been written in letters of blood. Through many generations, it

* "Antona's Banks." (1797.)

brought to its princely possessors a heritage of misery and bloodshed. Balliol, York, Plantagenet, and Stuart alike found in Fotheringhay a troubled home, a gloomy prison, or the scene of violent death; and Queen Elizabeth—who visited Fotheringhay in 1573—may, perhaps, have had its gruesome antecedents in her mind, when she selected Fotheringhay as the last prison of her lovely and hapless cousin, the Queen of Scots.

CHAPTER II.

Queen Elizabeth's visit to Fotheringhay.—James the First and his supposed "filial justice."—A vulgar error.—The Castle standing in 1625.—The survey of it.—The curse of King James.—Fuller's visit.—Dismantling of the Castle.—Its possessors.—Crown land.—Lord Overstone.—Decadence of the town.

Up to this last chapter of its history, Fotheringhay had doomed its princely tenants to more or less of misery; and the majority of the royal personages who were connected with it appear, either in their own persons or in those of their nearest relatives, to have met their ends by violent deaths. [Its history was written in characters of blood; and it would almost seem as if the tragical associations that thronged its towers should cause Queen Elizabeth (who had visited the castle in 1573, and had busied herself by putting up new monuments in the church to the slaughtered Dukes of York) to deliberately select Fotheringhay as the *last* prison of her regal victim, and as a fortress over whose portals might have been written, "All hope abandon, ye who enter here."] It is, at any rate, a noteworthy circumstance that, in the words of Mr. Nichols,* "Fotheringhay has been distinguished

* The distinguished historian of Leicestershire. See his "History and Antiquities of Fotheringhay," p. v., 1787—a scarce work, but, for the most part, embodied in the popular "Historic Notices of Fother-

beyond any other place in Britain, except the capital, by the aggravated misfortunes of royalty;" and its tragical records found their consummation in that dread event which, as it were, overwhelmed the castle with so great a shame that nothing less than its complete annihilation would answer the demands of poetic justice.

Probably some such feeling as this existed from the first, and gave a colourable pretext to the popular story (which is even entertained by Nichols and other historians), that no sooner had James I come to the throne than he caused Fotheringhay Castle to be demolished, in order to efface all traces of his mother's execution. The local poet who, in 1797, wrote the poem of "Antona's Banks,"* thus enshrines the vulgar error in his verse:

> "In darkest night for ever veil the scene
> When thy cold tomb received the captive Queen:
> For this has Time erased thee from his page,
> And filial justice, with vindictive rage,
> Burst on thy princely towers with whelming tide,
> Nor left one vestige to relate thy pride."

---

inghay," by the late Archdeacon Bonney. See also Bridge's "History of Northamptonshire," and Miss Strickland's "Queens of Scotland," vii. 420.

* The river Nene was sometimes called Avon. See Leland's "Itinerary," vol. i., fol. 4-6. "Foderingey stondithe on the farther rise of Avon, as I entered the towne. The bridge to Foderingey over Avon is of timber. The castelle of Foderingey is fair and meately strong, with doble ditches, and hath a kepe very auncient and strong. There be very fair lodgyns in the castel. And as I hard Catharine of Spaine did great costs in late tyme of refreshing of it. This castel longid of late tymes to Edmunde of

Even in a carefully-compiled book of reference by an eminent man—"The English Archæologist's Handbook: by Henry Godwin, F.S.A.," (Parker, 1867,) the vulgar error is repeated; for, mentioning Fotheringhay Castle, Mr. Godwin says, "Razed to the ground by James I." (p. 200.) Britton and Brayley (1807,) say of the castle, "On the accession of James to the throne of England, an order was issued for its demolition." (p. 218.) Samuel Lewis, in his "Topographical Dictionary," (1835,) says of Fotheringhay, "James I on his accession to the throne, demolished the castle." And this statement is commonly repeated in Guide-books and educational works. *

Archdeacon Bonney, the historian of Fotheringhay, in speaking of the destruction of the castle, says, "Thus removed by degrees it escaped the notice of the antiquary, who probably had recorded its destruction had it been less gradual." And, he adds, "The tale of its having been destroyed by order of James, on account of its having been

---

Langeley, Edward the iijd's sunne, and so lineally to the Dukes of York." The Warwickshire Avon takes its rise in Northamptonshire, but has not any connection with the Nene.

* For example, in the six-volume edition of Pinnock's *County Histories*, it says of Fotheringhay, "On the accession of James I. it was levelled with the ground. It was demolished by him because it had been the scene of the sufferings and death of his mother, the beauteous and unfortunate (perhaps criminal) Mary, Queen of Scots, who was imprisoned and beheaded here, by order of Queen Elizabeth." In the map of Northamptonshire given in this work, Fotheringhay is not marked.

the scene of his mother's suffering is clearly disproved; and must be left to those only who are fond of seeing events clothed in the language of fiction." The Archdeacon's work was printed and published by Mr. Thomas Bell, of Oundle, in 1821; and, it is not a little singular, that when Mr. T. Bell, published, in 1853, a volume of poems, "The Rural Album," with descriptive and "historical notices of Barnwell and Fotheringhay Castle," he wrote the following lines in a poem "On Fotheringhay Castle":

"Ah! let the grave conceal thine errors, Queen!
'Twas not thine errors, but thy charms, I ween,
That fir'd a cruel rival's vengeful hate
To spurn thy prayers, and leave thee to thy fate,
Who woman's tears, and kindred ties withstood,
And stain'd the annals of her reign with blood!

For this, ill-faited Castle! filial love
Struck down thy tow'rs, as vengeance from above,
Raz'd thy strong walls, from whose embattled side
The white rose banner wav'd in warlike pride,
And where the crook-backed king his vassals met,
And nobles hail'd the proud Plantagenet!"

But, in his "Historical Notices" of Fotheringhay, Mr. Bell says, "It has been said that James the First ordered the demolition of this castle; but, whether this was so or not, it is certain that in the last year of King James' reign it was surveyed, and its condition fully reported, and that soon after it was consigned to ruin."

FOTHERINGHAY.

It was not, then, "filial love" that struck down the tower of Fotheringhay and razed its strong walls. Unfortunately for those who would desire this story to be true, King James did nothing half so poetical or full of sympathetic "filial justice." On the contrary, although the castle would appear to have been uninhabited after the execution of Mary Stuart, and up to the end of Elizabeth's reign, yet no sooner had James ascended the throne than he turned the castle to account by bestowing it on some of his courtiers. He gave it to three proprietors; and when the first of these three (Lord Mountjoy, Earl of Devonshire) died, the other two (Sir Edward Blount and Joseph Earth, Esq.) conveyed the castle and lordship to his natural son, Mountjoy, who was afterwards created Earl of Newport. King James died on March 27th, 1625; and that the castle was standing in its integrity at that date is fully proved from the survey made on April 3rd, 1625, when it was thus described:—"The castle is a capital house, built of stone, moated with a double moat. A fair court within the castle; a building upon a mount, eight or sixteen square, with lower and upper chambers, to ascend by stairs, and then descending towards the hall, which is large and spacious. On the left hand the court is the chapel, and goodly lodgings; the great dining-room well garnished at present with pictures; next the hall are the buttery and kitchen; and, at the other end of the kitchen, a convenient yard for wood, with large beer-houses and back-houses, and offices. From the gate going out of the yard, there is a great yard half encompassing the castle, going round about to the first gate, and a great barn in the west side of the said yard; a gate house, and another ruinous house in the east corner of the same. The river Nene on the south side serves for the outer moate, and the mill-brooke on the east for the inner moate; between the mill-brooke and the castle was a great pond. The gate and fore-front of the house looks full north; and as soon as you are passed the inner drawbridge, at the gate there are some stairs leading up to some fair lodgings, and up higher into the wardrobe, and so to the fetter-lock on the top of the mount, on the north-west corner of the castle, which is built round of eight or sixteen square, with chambers as above." There is nothing said of demolition in this survey; and it is self-evident that, if James was inspired with that "filial revenge" which popular tradition has ascribed to him, he would have demolished Fotheringhay as soon as he had the power to do so. The popular tradition, indeed, goes still farther than the castle, and includes the whole town of Fotheringhay in the devastating mandate of King James. He laid a curse upon the town, and would have it burnt stick and stone, says the legend ; and it is in consequence of this curse (at any rate the people think so) that so many alarming fires have happened in the village. Yet, in the teeth of popular tradition, this fact stands clear, that Mary Stuart's son reigned twenty-two years, and that Fotheringhay Castle was standing after his death, and was then "a capital house," with its great dining-hall well garnished with pictures. This fact overrides the statement of those who, although rejecting the popular tradition, yet say (as was said at the meeting of the Archæological Institute at Peterborough in August, 1861, and at the meeting of the Lincoln and Northampton Society in September, 1859) that the castle having fallen into decay, and James having no use for it, he did not care to repair it.

And, indeed, did not Fuller the historian visit the castle, and there (as he tells us) read the following couplet from an old ballad* written on one of the windows with a diamond by the Queen of Scots herself?—

"From the top of all my trust,
Mishap hath laid me in the dust."

Now, as Fuller was not born till the year 1608, when James had already been king for five years, we have here another proof of his filial revenge, if ever exercised upon the destruction of Fotheringhay, was at any rate allowed to

* It is preserved in Ellis's "Specimens."

slumber for many years after he had the power of gratifying his desires. Fuller was born within ten miles of Fotheringhay, at the rectory-house of Aldwinkle, All Saints, the adjoining parish to Aldwinkle, St. Peter's, in whose rectory-house the poet Dryden was born; so that he probably visited the castle somewhere about the time when the survey was made in 1625, in which year, being then of the age of seventeen, Fuller took his B.A. degree at Cambridge. That survey, taken after the death of King James, does not make special mention of the castle being out of repair, or in a ruinous condition, except with some of the buildings in the court-yard. We are, however, driven to the presumption that the general condition of the castle was such that the expense of restoring it to its former grandeur so alarmed its then possessor, Mountjoy, Earl of Newport, that he preferred to dismantle the building and dispose of the materials.

Mountjoy died in the garrison at Oxford, Feb. 12, 1645, and was succeeded in his title by his only surviving son Henry, the last Earl of Newport, who died in 1679, without ever having enjoyed the estate, which (as appears from a deed preserved in the Fotheringhay church-chest, and printed by Nichols in the Appendix to his book) had been alienated by his father to Sir George Savile, of Thornhill, in the county of York, Bart., afterwards Marquis of Halifax. His son and successor, William, the second marquis, dying without male issue in 1700, the manor and lordship was sold by his father-in-law, Daniel, Earl of Nottingham, and the other trustees for the marquis's three co-heiresses, to Hewer Edgeley Hewer, Esq., who died, without issue, Nov. 16th, 1728, when it descended to the family of Blackburne. It then passed through several hands, until it was purchased by the Messrs. Belsey; and from Thomas Belsey, Esq., the survivor of the two purchasers, it passed to Robert Sacket Tomlin, Esq., of Dane Court, Kent, who sold it to Lord Overstone.

The late Mr. John Gough Nichols, F.S.A., told me that there was considerable delay in the completion of the purchase of Fotheringhay, respecting its validity; and that an old inhabitant of the place said to him, "Fotheringhay has had many masters; but, it's Crown land, and it'll go to the Crown again."

It will have been noticed that many of the owners of Fotheringhay died without male issue. This was the case of its late owner, who was, perhaps, the wealthiest of her Majesty's subjects. As Mr. Samuel Jones Loyd, the head of the banking firm, Jones, Loyd, and Co., he was raised to the Peerage, in 1850, as Baron Overstone of Overstone and Fotheringhay, in the County of Northampton. He had married, in 1829, Harriet, third daughter of Mr. Ichabod

Wright, of Mapperley Hall, Notts., and was left a widower with one child, a daughter, Harriet Sarah, born in 1837, who was married to Sir Robert James Lindsay, K.C.B., who has taken the prefix surname of Loyd. Lord Overstone died November 17th, 1883, at his residence in Carlton Gardens, in his 81st year; and, as he had no son, the title expired with him. He was the author of at least 28 publications, chiefly Letters, Remarks, Reflections, Reports, &c., on Decimal Coinage, Commerce, Bank Acts, Metallic and Paper Currency, the National Debt, &c.; but I am not aware that he ever wrote anything concerning Fotheringhay.

Nor do I know the precise date of Lord Overstone's purchase of Fotheringhay, but, it was some years previous to November, 1865; and, at that date, an inhabitant of the dwindling town told me that its owner had only once visited the spot. He said, "The property does not pass from father to son; and, during the last half century, it has been in possession of three families. The place is gradually becoming of smaller importance and proportions. In my early days, Fotheringhay could boast of two respectable inns, and a cattle and horse fair of considerable importance was held here. Now, it has not a beer shop or house of entertainment where a belated traveller or visitor can rest or refresh himself with a glass of home-brewed. Every farm and every house has changed its occupant more than once during my short sojourn. There is not a farmer can say,

> "I could trace out the time, a far distant date,
> When my grandfather toil'd in the field."

Trade diminishes in like proportion. Thirty years ago there were three or four families of stone-masons; they are now extinct, and there is no tailor, butcher, or shoemaker. Even the farm labourers are, for the most part, a new race during the last fifty years. It would, of course, be superstition to imagine that the curse of James still lingers on the spot; but, it appears to be overhung by "a gloom"; and this expression I have heard repeatedly from visitors, many of whom we see during the course of a season. But, whether it is from the malediction of King James, or some other cause, I do not pretend to know. I should rather attribute its decay to the want of some resident family of distinction to watch over the welfare, and to alleviate the wants, of those who require assistance."

CHAPTER III.

Sir Robert Bruce Cotton.—Conington Castle.—Sir Robert's birth at Denton.—His monument in Conington Church.—The Church and Mansion at Denton.—Sir Robert purchases a portion of Fotheringhay Castle.—The removal to Conington of various relics.

THE sadly matter-of-fact statement relative to the demolition of Fotheringhay Castle, is altogether out of harmony with the more poetical version of popular tradition; but, although it annihilates the pleasing evidence of James's filial affection, it paves the way for a record of an act precisely opposite in its nature by a more distant relative of Mary, Queen of Scots. This was Sir Robert Bruce Cotton, Bart., (so well known as the founder of the Cottonian Library, given to the British Museum by his grandson, Sir John Cotton,) who, being descended from the royal family of Scotland, was of kin to Mary Stuart. The relationship was recognised by King James, who, when Sir Robert appeared at court, was wont to address him as "cousin," and Sir Robert was not a little proud (as well he might be) of his royal ancestors, although he took a somewhat remarkable way of showing and publicly airing his connection with them by erecting complimentary monuments to their memory at Conington Church, Huntingdonshire, where they may be seen, together with his own monument and others to various members of the family.

If King James, according to popular tradition, was so desirous (which he was not) of annihilating every vestige of the scene of his mother's murder, it is evident that her cousin, Sir Robert Bruce Cotton—who, happily for posterity, had a collector's love of accumulating and preserving anything and everything on which he could lay hands—was equally anxious to treasure any memorials of that eventful transaction. Therefore, when Mountjoy, Earl of Newport, dismantled Fotheringhay Castle, and disposed of its materials, Sir Robert Cotton seized upon the golden opportunity of acquiring a memento of his "cousin's" execution. At this time Sir Robert had been living (when he was not at Cotton House, Westminster) at the family mansion in the little village of Denton, Huntingdonshire, where he was born on January 22, 1571, and which, as the crow flies, is not seven miles distant from Fotheringhay; and he was desirous of building a new mansion on his Conington estate about three miles from Denton, on the other side of the great north road. Conington had come to the Cottons through the Bruces, having descended to them from David I, who had married the widow of Simon de St. Liz, who built Fotheringhay Castle; so that there was a strong link of connection between Conington and Fotheringhay long before it was strengthened by Sir Robert Bruce Cotton.

How Sir Robert came to be born at Denton, and not at Conington, is told in Collins' "Baronetage of England" from whence the account has been more briefly copied by Wotton, the *Biographia Britannica*, the writer of the life prefixed to Smith's and Planta's "Catalogue of the Cottonian Library," and others. The passage is quaint, and runs thus:—"Robert, only son by the first wife, was born 22. Jan., A.D. 1570, in the village of Denton, near Conington (part of his Ancestor's Inheritance), his Parents having removed thither not long after their marriage, as well for the splendour of his Birth, as to be more at liberty from the incommodiousness of their own Seat, arising from a great Accession of new Domesticks."* So that, even then, servants would seem to have been considered one of the greatest plagues of life.

In the year 1852, being then Curate of Glatton-with-Holme, the two parishes lieing between Denton and Caldecote, I copied the inscription of Sir Robert Bruce Cotton's birth, from the Denton register, and of his funeral, from the Conington register, and exhibited these, with water-colour drawings of the ancient font in Denton Church, and Sir Robert's

* Ed. 1720; p. 197. Fuller was wrong in stating that he was "born at Cunnington."

tomb in Conington Church, before one of the meetings of the Royal Society of Antiquaries, in London. Subsequently, I was Rector of Denton and Caldecote for twelve years—from 1859 to 1871; so that I had every reason to take a special interest in Sir Robert Bruce Cotton, of Denton and Conington, and of his connection with Fotheringhay. The register of his birth in the Denton register is as follows:—

> "A. Dni. 1571. Mr. Robert Cotton was borne ye XXIJ of January and baptized ye XXVI of ye same."

The register is at the foot of the page, and is attested by the names of "William Garfit, Rect., & Ro^t. Clarke & Williã Swift," with the monograms of the Churchwardens. The register of his funeral at Conington is as follows:—"Ano Dom. 1631. S^r. Robert Cotton, Baronett, sepult fuit XXIIJ^o die Maij." He had died at his house in Westminster, but was buried at Conington, by his own request, in the south chapel of the Nave, close under the spot where his portrait-bust in marble hands down his features to generations who have profited by his well-timed and well-directed labours. The precise spot underneath which he is laid, is marked by a slab, bearing the inscription, "S^r. R. C., May 13, 1631." In the inscription on the monument, the date of his birth is given "Natus XXII. Januarii MDLXX.," which makes a discrepancy with the "1571" of the Denton register. We have to bear in mind, however, that the commencement of the civil year was in March.

Sir Robert Bruce Cotton rebuilt the little church of All Saints, Denton, in 1620, as is recorded in a stone over the east window. He carefully preserved the curious Norman tower, the early south doorway, and the late Norman hexagonal font in which he had been baptised. His grandson, Sir John Cotton—the donor to the nation of "the Cottonian manuscripts"—built the outer porch to the church, bearing date 1665.* Subsequently, the interior of the church fell into great decay, from which I was able to rescue it, during the time I had the living. In re-pewing the church, as much of the old oak was preserved as was possible, including a bench end on which was carved the date "1607." From the Cottonian manuscripts, it appears that there was, formerly, in the east window of Denton church "a shield of arms displaying quarterly: first, Cotton; second, Bruce; third, Scot; and fourth, Earl Waltheof."

The mansion-house of the Cottons, at Denton, stood on the land adjoining the south side of the churchyard, on the precise spot now occupied by a barn and farm-buildings.

* Mr. W. Caveler, the writer of Part V. of Parker's "Ecclesiastical and Architectural Topography of England," (1851,) is misled by this date, and ascribes the whole of the re-building of the Church to that period. Brayley and others had previously made the same misstatement.

The base of the barn is a part of the foundation of the mansion, which, having fallen into a ruinous state, was pulled down, about the year 1816, by the Lord of the Manor, Admiral Wells, of Holme-wood House. I have had the three-storied mansion described to me by persons who well remembered it; and I traced, through various possessors, some furniture that had belonged to the house —a carved oak bedstead, a carved oak cabinet, and two carved oak chairs, on which was the royal crown—a badge of which the cousin of King James and Mary, Queen of of Scots was not a little proud. When I first knew the spot, there were other traces of the old mansion-house and its garden and three fish-ponds; but when, in 1855, a new farm-house was built, the ground was levelled, two fish-ponds were filled up, and other alterations were made. Three of the fields attached to this farm still bear the names of "Cotton's Close," "Cotton Meadow," and "Cotton Hill," the last named being on the brow of the hill between Denton and Stilton.

As Sir Robert Bruce Cotton died on May 6th, 1631, and as the survey (already mentioned) of Fotheringhay Castle, was made on April 3rd, 1625, a week after the death of the King, we may, probably, refer the demolition of Fotheringhay to about the year 1626 or 7. It would appear that, at whatever date this demolition occurred, Sir Robert Bruce Cotton took advantage of it to purchase certain portions of Fotheringhay to incorporate them into the additions that he was making to Conington Castle; and he would seem to have been chiefly influenced in doing this, not so much for the sake of the material, but in order that he might add to his castle some substantial relics of that other castle, in which his lovely and ill-starred royal cousin had met her doom.

For this purpose, he purchased the banquetting-hall, which had been the scene of her execution. This consisted, for the most part, of the eleven arches and columns that are placed on the exterior of the north and west fronts of the ground floor of Conington Castle, but which, most probably, stood in the interior of the Fotheringhay banquetting-hall, dividing it into three aisles. This was an arrangement often to be seen in large halls of important castles; an excellent specimen of which exists in the ancient hall of Oakham Castle, where the horse-shoes are now hung. The original Westminster Hall, as stated in Parker's "Domestic Architecture of England"—is supposed to have been of this form; as was also the Bishop's Hall at Lincoln. The lodgings occupied by the unfortunate Queen of Scots are believed to have been the same as those in which Queen Elizabeth was lodged, when, in one of her progresses, she visited Fotheringhay, and, on observing in the choir the ruinous state of the monuments of her ancestors, the Dukes of York, directed that their bodies should be removed into the present church, and buried on either side of the communion table, aud that proper monuments should be erected to their memory. It seems "an irony of fate," that the two Queens should have occupied the same rooms during their sojourn at Fotheringhay.

CHAPTER IV.

The Banquet-hall of Fotheringhay removed to Conington.—J. M. Heathcote, Esq.—His ancestors, and their purchase of Conington from the Cottons.—The chair from which Mary, Queen of Scots is believed to have risen for execution.—Contemporary accounts.—Other remains of Fotheringhay.—The Talbot Inn, Oundle.—Chapel at Fineshade.—Thorough destruction of the Castle.

"Sir Robert Bruce Cotton"—according to Camden, who was his personal friend—"brought from Fotheringhay the whole room where Mary, Queen of Scots was beheaded."* The entrance porch at Conington Castle is also believed to have been brought from Fotheringhay, together with two handsome pillars, surmounted by carved stone coronets, which are placed on either side of the entrance gates on the Great North Road. Two autotype plates of Conington Church and Castle, in 1800, and in 1875, from original drawings by John Moyer Heathcote, Esq., of Conington Castle, will be found in that gentleman's illustrated volume, "Fen and Mere"; † and in the latter of the two illustrations, the columns and arches from the Fotheringhay banquetting-hall are plainly seen, together with the entrance porch.

---

* See Camden's *Britannia.* (Vol. II. "Iceni"; ed. 1789.)

† Published by Longmans, 1876, price 28s. The arches, porch, &c. are also shewn in a line engraving, from a drawing by J. P. Neale, published by Jones and Co., Finsbury Square, London, Oct. 9, 1830.

Conington Castle would appear not to have been well-cared for by Sir Robert Bruce Cotton's immediate successors; for, his great-grandson, Sir John Cotton, found it to be in so ruinous a state, that—preferring to live at his other seat, Stratton in Bedfordshire—he took down the greater part of the castle, but left standing that portion that included the remains of the banquet-hall from Fotheringhay. When Dr. Stukely visited Conington, in 1724, he "was concerned to see a stately old house, of hewn stone, large and handsome, in dismal ruins. The deserted *lares* and genius of the place had fled. A poor cottage or two seemed to be the whole town, once in possession of the Kings of Scotland." It is a singular coincidence that relics of the Queen of Scots should have been transported to this Scottish "town of kings"—which is the meaning of the word Conington.

The manor of Conington was purchased of the heirs of Sir Robert Bruce Cotton, for the sum of £2,500, in the year 1753, by Sir John Heathcote,* from whom the present

* Sir John Heathcote was the son of Sir Gilbert Heathcote, a man of great note. He was one of the founders of the Bank of England, and was the last Lord Mayor of London who rode on horseback in the procession on Lord Mayor's day. He was the "Sir Andrew Freeport" of *The Spectator*; is mentioned by Pope (*Imitations of Horace*; Book II., Ep. 2, l. 240,)

"Heathcote himself, and such large-acred men";

and appears in Bramble's *Letter* and Dyer's *Fleece*:

"And such the grassy slopes and verdant lawns
Of beauteous Normanton, health's pleasing haunts,
And the beloved retreat of Heathcote's leisure."

Lord Aveland is lineally descended. Sir John's grandson, John Heathcote (who was born in 1767, and married to Mary Ann Thornhill in 1799,) restored Conington Castle, in 1800—1813, from designs by Cockerell, the grounds being laid out by Lappidge. Further additions were made, in 1833, under the direction of Blore, by Mr. John Moyer Heathcote, who also employed Blore in the restoration of the church, which stands close to the castle. The tall tower of the church, with its four-light transomed windows, richly panelled battlement, and octagonal crocketed pinnacles, is well seen by the traveller on the Great Northern railway.

In the chancel of Conington Church, is a large and finely-carved Abbot's chair, said by Gough, in his "Additions to Camden," to have formerly belonged to Peterborough, and to have been seen by Lord Coleraine in Conington Church, in the year 1743. This chair is traditionally said to have been that which was provided for the Queen of Scots on the scaffold, and in which she sat to hear the reading of her death-warrant. It may have been sent to Fotheringhay from Peterborough; and, on the demolition of Fotheringhay, removed to Conington by Sir Robert Bruce Cotton. The nature of the decorations of the chair would seem to show

He was Knighted by Queen Anne, and created a Baronet in 1733. He is buried at Normanton, where is his portrait. Another portrait is in the dining-room at Conington Castle.

THE CHAIR FROM WHICH MARY, QUEEN OF SCOTS, IS BELIEVED TO HAVE RISEN FOR EXECUTION.

that it was used for religious purposes, on the south side of the altar; as the figures of the four angels, and of the two ecclesiastical figures holding books, that ornament the top and sides of the chair, all face sideways, which would be facing to the east. The figures of the four angels bear musical instruments. Another angel is carved in one of the spandrels at the back of the chair; the other spandrel representing the Virgin Mary, crowned as Queen of Heaven, with her hand raised in benediction, and her emblematic pot of lilies at her feet. At the base of the chair is a band of quatrefoils, carved in high relief. This handsome chair, carefully preserved in Conington Church, is believed to be a mute memorial of that tragic scene in which it once played its part.

From the accounts of the various historians, there would appear to have been three chairs placed on the scaffold in the banquet-hall at Fotheringhay; two of these were for the Earls of Kent and Shrewsbury; and the other, covered with black cloth, with a cushion of black velvet before it, was reserved for the Queen of Scots; and, on that chair she sat, looking around her smiling, with absolute composure, no muscle quivering in her face, while she listened to Beale, the Clerk of the Council, reading the warrant against her—though, it is said, that she listened to it as though it no ways concerned her, and (as Froude says) "in all the assembly Mary Stuart appeared the least interested in the words which were consigning her to death." If, as is quite probable, this memorable scene occurred when the Queen of Scots was sitting in the very chair that is now preserved in Conington Church, then we see in it a relic of the first importance in connection with the fatal tragedy of Fotheringhay; and, it can readily be imagined that Sir Robert Bruce Cotton, Mary Stuart's cousin, would desire to possess this relic, together with the stones of the hall in which, so bravely, she suffered her cruel death.

One of the witnesses of that execution was a person whose initials, "R. W." only are disclosed to us. His account is preserved in the Harleian Manuscripts, and has been given in full by Camden, Nichols, Bonney and others. He makes mention only of "a lowe stoole" on which she sat, and from which, presently, she "began to slide," while the Dean of Peterborough was pestering her with his tedious address; for, she was saying her own prayers, and this brought her upon her knees, upon "the faire long cushion" provided for her. This "stoole"—if thereby a seat without a back is signified—may have been in addition to the chair. The contemporary painting of the execution, represented in miniature in the back-ground of the Windsor Castle portrait of Mary, Queen

STAIRCASE AND WINDOW, TALBOT INN, OUNDLE.

of Scots, dressed for the scaffold, does not particularly help us to a solution of this point; for, although it certainly does not show a high chair—and there should be three—it also omits the black-covered rails round the scaffold, and conveys an erroneous idea of its dimensions. It also does not assist us to any idea of the architecture of the hall; but, on this point, we do not depend upon the slippery ground of traditionary evidence, and are enabled to look upon the series of eleven pillars and arches of Conington Castle as a veritable portion of the banquetting-hall of Fotheringhay.

Traditionary evidence—and, I fear, that alone—can assist us to some other details of the hall. That very interesting specimen of domestic architecture, the Talbot Inn at Oundle, is said to have been built from the stones of Fotheringhay; and its great staircase window, looking into the yard, is believed to have once lighted the Fotheringhay banqueting-hall; the wide oaken staircase, and the great entrance-gates, with their ponderous bolts and ironwork, (lately replaced by new gates) are also supposed to have been brought from the castle. Other portions were used by Robert Kirkham, Esq. for the erection of a chapel at Fineshade, and for various buildings in the immediate neighbourhood; and since then, even up to the present day, the scattered remains of the castle, even to the very foundations, have been used for the repair of the navigation of the river, for the renovation of dilapidated farm-buildings, and for all those miscellaneous and useful purposes to which blocks of stone can be applied. It may, therefore, readily be imagined that any one who visits Fotheringhay with the expectation of seeing what are commonly called "ruins" will be woefully disappointed. All that such an one will see will be the mound on which the keep once stood, the inequalities of the ground where the various divisions of the castle have been, and one solitary and shapeless block of masonry (measuring somewhere about six by nine feet in thickness, and seven feet high) which has tumbled over on its side, not far from the river's edge, and has there been permitted to remain as the sole survivor of a destruction more sweeping and complete than almost any other in England's annals of baronial architecture.

"Ill-omened spot! where are thy glories now?
Where the gay helmet and the plumes of snow?
Where now the train of gallant warriors? where
The Royal victim and her sable bier?
All gone alike; no relic left to tell
Here Richard dwelt, and here Queen Mary fell!
Yet still the muse in sad historic song
To future ages shall the tale prolong,
Revive the bloody deed in mournful lay;
And, though the saddening scene has pass'd away,
The feeling heart shall grieve the tale to hear,
And Mary's cruel death shall claim a tear!"*

* "On Fotheringhay Castle," in "The Rural Album," by Thomas Bell, of Barnwell. (J. Masters, London: 1853.)

REMAINS OF FOTHERINGHAY CASTLE.

CHAPTER V.

Fotheringhay village, ancient and modern.—The New Inn.—Its history. The Market-stead.—Relick Sunday.—The Cross.—The May-pole. —The Bridge.—Queen Elizabeth.—The Collegiate Church.—Distant view.—Archdeacon Bonney's work on Fotheringhay.

FOTHERINGHAY itself, although reduced from its original importance of a Northamptonshire market town, and as the seat of the proud Plantagenets, still presents much the same appearance that it did in Leland's day; for it "is but of one street, all of stone building," and "the glorie of it standeth by the paroche church of a fair buildid and collegiated," and "there be exceeding goodly meadows," and "mervelus fair corn ground and pasture, but little woodde." The village at the present day consists of a long, straggling street, on a gentle rise above the northern bank of the winding river Nene. The houses are wholly built of stone, and many of them are thatched; those at the eastern end of the street, towards the castle, are called the Old and New Inns, the former having long since been converted into a number of small tenements. The New Inn still remains in much of its integrity; and, with its large Gothic arch, decorated with roses, quatrefoils, and armorial bearings of the Yorks and of Edward IV, affords an excellent example of the domestic architecture of the time of that monarch. From the survey taken in 1624, it appears that this New Inn had two fair courts and a back part with barns and stables; the chief portion of the building "containing a hall, a parlour, a kitchen, and divers other chambers." Galleries ran round the inner court. The building was probably erected by King Edward IV, for, on shields to the right and left of the window over the entrance gateway, and also of the gateway itself, four generations, in succession, are represented: (1) Castile and Leon, for Isabel, wife of Edmund of Langley, younger daughter of Peter, King of Castile and Leon, and mother of the Earl of Cambridge; (2) Mortimer, for the Countess of Cambridge, mother of Richard, Duke of York; (3) Nevile of Raby, for Richard, Duke of York and his Duchess, Cicely; and (4) a shield bearing France and England, quarterly, for Edward IV. When Sir Amyas Paulet conducted the Queen of Scots to Fotheringhay, this New Inn housed some of his two thousand horse-soldiers, who were billeted there and at various houses in the village; and the commissioners and judges at Mary's mock trial were also put up at the New Inn. Those who attended the funeral of Richard, Duke of York, would also, for the most part, be quartered at the New Inn. Its outer court and galleries have been removed, and its interior greatly altered and modernised for the purposes of a farm-house of the better class.

The old "Market-stead," as it was called, was at the open space at the north-west corner of the churchyard; and the privilege of the market, and of the annual fair held on Michaelmas-eve and the two following days, is mentioned, in a grant given to the Earl of Richmond, in the year 1309. The grant was afterwards confirmed by Richard, Duke of York, and the time of holding the fair was transferred to the day after "Relick Sunday,"* the anniversary of Thomas a'Becket. Though the fair—after a fashion—still remains, the market would appear to have lapsed into disuse in the time of Edward IV.

It is possible that the cross stood in this spot; though it may have stood in White-Cross field, to the west of the town. It was destroyed in 1580. It is clearer that the Maypole stood here; for, in the ancient manuscript "book of the affairs of the parish," there is an entry, under date 1578, of a sum paid to a carpenter for "squaring the Maypole that stands in the Market-steede." Squaring a Maypole must have been pleasanter and more profitable work than squaring a circle.

When the Queen of Scots was brought from Chartley, in Staffordshire, in September, 1586, under the charge of Sir Amyas Paulet, she entered Fotheringhay by the bridge over

* The Sunday after the 7th of July.

the Nene, that had recently been built by the Queen of England. It was a stone bridge of four arches, following a gentle curve, and fenced with wooden piers. Previous to the erection of the bridge, the river Nene had to be crossed by a ford,* to guard which, the mound on which the castle was afterwards built, was raised by some Anglian or Danish possessor. A tablet was placed on the bridge, carved with the initials E. R., with a knot between them. Underneath which, was the following inscription :—

"God save the Queen.
"This Bridge was made by Queen
Elizabeth in the 15th yere of her Reygne.
A.D. 1573."

Thirteen years later, her victim was carried across that bridge to her last prison. Did she happen to see the inscription? A few more generations in the whirligig of time, and Cromwell's soldiers were hacking that inscription with their swords, and, in their zeal against monarchy, erased the words "God save the Queen." But, in process of time, the bridge required renewal, and it was re-built, in 1722, by George Portwood, a Stamford mason, of stone from the King Cliffe's quarry, by Daniel, Earl of Nottingham, and the trustees of William Savile, Marquis of Halifax, who were the proprietors of the estate. The navigation of the river Nene, was opened on

* This ford was in connection with an ancient road that ran from Ermine Street.

September 11th, 1728. It had been projected so long ago as the time of Edward IV, who came here by water, from Crowland, in 1469, to join his Queen, who was then in residence at Fotheringhay Castle.

The beautiful church of Fotheringhay is but a fragment of a great idea. It was designed to be a collegiate church; but its chancel, and the collegiate buildings, were destroyed in the last year of Edward VI. It is unnecessary to describe it here, further than to say that it consists of a nave with aisles, and a square tower supporting an octagonal lantern; pinnacles rise from the battlements of the aisles, and flying buttresses support the clerestories. The church contains the original font and pulpit (with Richard III's badge of the boar), and the monuments erected by Queen Elizabeth to the Dukes of York. They bear the badge of the falcon enclosed within a horse fetter-lock, which also appears on the summit of the church vane. The church, with its tower and octagon, makes a fine object in the view, as seen by the railway traveller, near to the Elton Station, on the line between Northampton and Peterborough. The castle mound can also be clearly seen. Any traveller who can spare the time for the four hours between trains, would do well to stop at Elton Station, and make his way to Fotheringhay, which is but a mile-and-a-half distant across the fields. It is a pleasant walk, and the church tower will be his guide. He will be able, on his way, to quote the author of "The Forest," and say,

"Before me winding pathways lead
To upland lawn and level mead;
Where Nene in silent sorrow laves
The princely Warriors' lowly graves,
And that dismantled Mount where stood
The Towers imbued with Stuart's blood."

On his route, he will see, on the other side of the river, "the exceeding goodly meadowes by Foderinghey," of which Leland speaks, and which gave the name to the place—the "hay," "eye," or inclosure of the foddering meadow. In process of time, "Foderinghey" was more mellifluously pronounced Fotheringhay. In the Domesday book it appears as "Fodringeia."

The best and most complete description of this beautiful church will be found in Mr. Parker's tract, "Some Remarks upon the Church of Fotheringhay" (1841), illustrated by thirty-one woodcuts, and containing a copy of the original contract for building the church, in the 13th of Henry VI, 1435. This contract is one of the few original documents of this kind that have been preserved to us from the Middle Ages, and affords some curious and interesting information, which Mr. Parker has explained and illustrated throughout from the building itself.

Archdeacon Bonney's well-known book on Fotheringhay has long been out of print, and is now somewhat scarce.* With great industry and painstaking, he obtained the sources of his materials, from ancient manuscripts in his own, and the Vicar's possession; the Harleian collection; Records in the Chapter-house, Westminster; Bridge's History of Northamptonshire; Rymer's "Fœdera," and other works, especially an unpublished Record of Dugdale in the possession of George Finch Hatton, Esq. Archdeacon Bonney's account of Fotheringhay Church occupies twenty-five pages, exclusive of his description of the College and its dissolution; but, it will be sufficient for the purpose of this handbook if the following abbreviated description is given; referring to the Archdeacon's work for the fuller account, together with its views of the Church, and the plates of shields.

* "Historic Notices in reference to Fotheringhay." Illustrated by Engravings. By the Rev. H. K. Bonney, M.A., author of the Life of Bishop Taylor. Oundle: Printed by and for T. Bell. London: Longman. Edinburgh: Constable. 1821.

CHAPTER VI.

Description of Fotheringhay Church.—The projected College.—Destruction of the Choir.—The Church tower and clere-story.—The bells.—The porch.—The fetterlock badge.—The font.—The pulpit.—Monuments to the Dukes of York.—Royal funerals.—The hero of Agincourt.—Burial of Richard, Duke of York.—Edward IV.

THE stately Church of Fotheringhay is, throughout, in the Perpendicular style, and, although but a fragment of the original idea, is an excellent specimen of the architecture of that period.

Edmund of Langley having projected the building of a college at Fotheringhay, began to fulfil his intentions by erecting "a large and magnificent choir," at the east end of the old parish church. And after his death, his son, Edward, Duke of York, wishing to rebuild the nave of the old church upon the same plan as the choir, appointed trustees for that purpose. The death of the Duke of York at Agincourt, put a stop to further proceedings; but the present church is a monument of the care with which the trust was afterwards fulfilled. The Duke did not live to see even the foundation of the building laid. The plan was carried into execution by his nephew and successor, Richard, Duke of York, through his Commissioners, who signed a

THE BRIDGE AND CHURCH, FOTHERINGHAY.

deed of agreement with "William Howard, a freemason of Fotheringhay," on the twenty-fourth day of September, in the thirteenth year of Henry VI, 1435. It is more than probable that the buildings were not completed till the time of Edward IV, who erected the cloister, which, for its superior elegance, was styled "the fair cloister;" the windows of which were enriched with painted glass.

In the year 1477, King Edward IV erected on the north side of the high altar, over the graves of his father, Richard, Duke of York, and his brother, Edmund, Earl of Rutland, a handsome shrine, which Leland describes as "a pratie chapelle," and Camden as "a magnificent monument."

The destruction of the choir and college may be dated from the last year of Edward VI, when they were granted to Dudley, Duke of Northumberland. The progress of their ruin was more gradual than has been represented; for part of the choir was standing in the reign of Elizabeth, and the glass was in the windows of the cloister and college hall, when Dugdale visited the spot in 1641. Of the shields of arms that were then remaining, Dugdale gives a minute description.

The windows of the nave and side aisles were also painted; and contained figures of saints, cardinals, and prelates. Above these were angels playing on various musical instruments; the Bohemian plume, and the falcon inclosed by a fetterlock, already mentioned as the device of the House of York. Whilst that powerful family was contending for the Crown, the falcon was represented as endeavouring to expand its wings, and force open the lock. When the family had actually ascended the throne, the falcon was represented as free, and the lock open. The western windows were ornamented with the rose, the white hart, the fetterlock, and the lion. "The whole," says Stukely, "were saved during the civil war by the minister of the parish, who bribed the soldiers to preserve them." Many of these figures were perfect in the year 1787; but, at present, not a window retains its former beauty.

The remains of the collegiate church exhibit an admirable specimen of the architecture of the fifteenth century. A tower of two stories rises above the west end of the nave. The lower story is square, and is finished with a plain parapet, ornamented at the angles with octagonal, embattled turrets. Upon these were originally placed figures that were, probably, the symbols of the four Evangelists; no uncommon ornament on the towers of churches. The sides of this part of the tower are pierced with three small and four larger windows, under obtuse-angled arches, and are divided by plain tracery. The upper story is octagonal, embattled, and adorned at the angles with crocketed pinnacles. In each of its sides is a lofty window of three lights, elegant tracery, and of more easy curvature than that of the windows in the tower below.

The clere-story of the church is strengthened by ten segments of arches, which spring from the top of the buttresses of the aisles; some of these are fallen into decay. The buttresses are finished with a pinnacle; and between each is a window of four lights, and handsome tracery. Both the aisles and the clere-story are embattled.

At the west end of the church, beneath the tower, is a spacious entrance, under an arch, within a square moulding, ornamented at the angles by an escutcheon in the centre of a quarter-foil. Above this is a large and lofty window, divided into fourteen lights, and finished with elegant tracery. There is also a window at the west end of the aisles, which projects westward, so as to be nearly even with the wall of the tower. The entrance under the tower is flanked by two bold and lofty buttresses.

The peal consists of four bells: round the first is inscribed, "*Thomas Norris made me, 1634.*" Round the second, "*Domini laudem, 1634, non verbo sed voce resonabo.*" Round the third, "*A. M. R. B. W. W. C. 4. 1609.*" Round the fourth, "*W. W. 1595. Praise God, H. B.*"

The entrance most in use is under a large plain porch, on the north side of the church. A similar porch stood on the south side, adjoining the south-eastern end of the aisle. This was the entrance from the college, that covered the eminence on the south of the churchyard. The wall, which now bounds the churchyard in that quarter, was the north side of the cloister.

The device of the fetterlock remained in most of the windows of the church, till the year 1807; and, it is retained to this day upon the point of the flag-pole on the tower.

Warton, in his *History of Poetry*, notices the church at Fotheringhay; and commends it as a specimen of bold and perfect style. He classes it with the divinity-school at Oxford, and the chapel of King's College, Cambridge. To the latter of these the groining and spandrels, beneath the tower, have a strong resemblance. Thence the nave, flanked by four arches, of simple but elegant construction, (which divide it from the aisles,) and terminated by a lofty arch and font beneath—presents a view of the edifice, as it existed in the time of its royal and munificent benefactor.

The length of the church from west to east is 87 feet, and the width 68 feet. The height of the nave beneath the tower, is 41 feet; of the tower, from the floor to the roof of the octagon, 133 feet 4 inches; and of the aisles 27 feet to the top of the battlement.

The font is an interesting object. The basin is octagonal, adorned with foliage and grotesque heads, within gothic compartments; and supported on a low octagonal pillar, and elevated upon two steps. On the west side of it is a stone pedestal, designed for the station of the priest, when he performs the office of baptism. Baptisteries are seldom found so conveniently arranged as this to give the congregation a complete view of the ceremony. At the great festivals, when a full congregation is in the nave, the sponsors are kneeling on the steps around, and the minister elevated in his proper place, the ability of the architect's design is the more visible and impressive.

The old seats in the area of the church were removed in 1817, when wainscot pews were substituted for them. The pulpit is original and in good preservation. It is hexagonal, supported on one pillar, and adorned with carved panels inserted in a border of tracery. Above are the remains of the canopy; which, generally, since the Reformation, has given place to a large sounding-board. On examining the canopy, whilst it was under repair, some of the ancient gilding was discovered. At the back is a shield of arms, bearing France and England quarterly; supported on the dexter side, by a lion rampant guardant, for the earldom of March; and a bull, for Clare; on the sinister, by a hart, showing the descent from Richard II., who took that device; and by a boar, for the honour of Windsor, possessed by Richard III. Gray, alluding to the murder of the Princes, characterizes Richard by this badge, and says,

The bristled boar, in infant gore,
Wallows beneath the thorny shade.

The shield of arms is surmounted by an imperial crown.

The memorials of the dead within these hallowed walls are numerous. The pavement contains many stones; but the brasses that once represented effigies, and recorded names and dates, have mostly disappeared; only one plate remaining.

There are, however, two regal monuments which merit especial notice, though rather from the rank of the personages than for architectural beauty. When Queen Elizabeth visited Fotheringhay, in one her progresses, she observed the graves of her ancestors, the Dukes of York, neglected amongst the ruins of the choir. She, therefore, commanded that their bodies should be removed into the present church, and deposited on each side the communion-table, giving directions to her treasurer, for monuments to be erected to their memory. On opening the graves, the bodies were found to to be inclosed in lead; and, round the neck of Cicely,

Duchess of York, was a silver ribbon, with a pardon from Rome, written in a fine Roman hand, "as fair and fresh" says Fuller, "as if it had been written yesterday."

The monuments are in the debased taste of that age, and ornamented with ducal coronets and falcons and fetterlocks. The one on the south side bears France and England quarterly, with a label of five points for Edward, Duke of York, who was slain at Agincourt; and, on the cornice, was a Latin inscription. The monument on the north side is a counterpart of the other, bearing France and England quarterly, with a label of five points, impaling a saltire, surmounted by a ducal coronet, for Richard, Duke of York, who was killed at Wakefield; and his Duchess, Cicely, daughter of Ralph Neville, first Earl of Westmorland. It is singular that there was no inscription on this monument to the memory of Edmund, Earl of Rutland, whose remains were interred in the same grave with those of his father.

Over each of the monuments is a wooden tablet. On the southern one is this inscription:—"Edward, Duke of York, was slain at the Battle of Agincourt, in the 3rd year of Henry the 5th, 1415." On the northern tablet is, "Richard Plantagenet, Duke of York, Nephew to Edward, Duke of York, and father to King Edward the 4th, was slain at Wakefield, in the 37th year of Henry the 6th, 1459: and lies buried here with Cicely, his wife.—Cicely, Duchess of York, was daughter to Ralph Neville, first Earl of Westmorland."

A few more details may be acceptable to the reader relative to the royal funerals at Fotheringhay.

The hero of Agincourt left directions for his funeral, ordering his body to be buried in the parochial church of Fotheringhay, in the midst of the choir, near the steps, under a flat marble. His body was, accordingly, brought over to England, and carried to Westminster; his exequies being solemnly performed by the archbishops and most of the bishops, by the king's order, in St. Paul's cathedral. From Westminster it was brought to Fotheringhay, and on Dec. 1, 1415, interred in the choir. The tomb is described by Leland, who saw it, as "a flat marble stone; and upon it was his image flat in brass."

Richard, Duke of York, fell in the battle of Wakefield.* His body was first interred at Pontefract, but afterwards removed, with that of his son Edmund, Earl of Rutland, in great pomp, to Fotheringhay. On July 22, 1466, their remains were put into a chariot, covered with black velvet,

* Queen Margaret set his head above Micklegate Bar,
"That York might overlook the town of York."
Edward IV removed the head of his father to Fotheringhay.

richly wrapped in cloth of gold and royal habit. At the feet of the duke stood the figure of an angel clothed in white, and bearing a crown of gold, to signify that of right he was a king. The chariot was drawn by seven horses, trapped to the ground, and covered with black, charged with escutcheons of that prince's arms. Every horse carried a man, and upon the foremost rode Sir John Skipwith, who bore the duke's banner displayed. The bishops and abbots, in their robes, went two or three miles before, to prepare the reception of the remains. Richard, Duke of Gloucester, followed next after the chariot, accompanied by several of the nobility and officers of arms. In this order, they left Pontefract, and that night rested at Doncaster, where they were received by the convent of Cordeliers, in grey habit. Thence by easy stages, they proceeded to Blithe, Tuxford in the Clay, Newark, Grantham, and Stamford; and on Monday, July 29, the procession reached Fotheringhay, where the bodies were received by several bishops and abbots in their robes, and supported by twelve servants of the deceased. At the entrance of the churchyard, King Edward IV, accompanied by several dukes, earls, and barons, in mourning, were in attendance, who proceeded to the choir of the church, near the high altar, where was a hearse covered with black, furnished with banners and other insignia. Upon this hearse were placed the remains of the duke and his son Edmund. The queen * and her two daughters were also present in mourning, attended by several ladies and other persons. Over the image was a cloth of majesty of black sarcenet; with the figure of our Lord sitting on a rainbow, of beaten gold, having in every corner an escutcheon of the arms of France and England quarterly; with a valence round the hearse also of deep, black sarcenet, fringed half a yard deep, and ornamented with three angels of beaten gold, holding the duke's arms within a garter, in every part above the hearse.

Upon the morrow, the 30th, several masses were said; and at the offertory of the mass of requiem, the king offered for the prince his father; and the queen, her two daughters, and the duchess (countess) of Richmond, offered afterwards. Then Norroy, king of arms, offered the prince's coat of arms; March, king of arms, the target; Ireland, king of arms, the sword; Windsor, herald of England, and Ravendon, herald of Scotland, offered the helmet; and Mr. de Ferreys, the harness and courser.

Edward, Earl of March, afterwards Edward IV, succeeded his father, both in the honours of his house and the possession of Fotheringhay Castle and lordship; Cicely, his mother, still

* Elizabeth, daughter of Sir Richard Woodville, and widow of Sir John Gray, Knight, who was killed at the battle of St. Albans.

retaining her right in it until the ninth year of his reign; when Guy Woolston, Esq., was appointed constable of the Castle of Fotheringhay, and keeper of the Great Park. Fotheringhay, from Leland's description, would seem to have been the favourite residence of this powerful and royal house; and the Duchess Cicely, who survived her husband thirty-four years, inhabited the castle during the greater part of her widowhood.

CHAPTER VII.

Fotheringhay Castle, the royal residence of York.—The Castle-keep.—Its shape.—View from the Church tower.—The Castle moats.—Buttressed wall.—Scarcity of illustrations of the Castle.—Mary Stuart albums.—Miss Agnes Strickland.—Joseph Cecil, Esq.—Schiller's "Mary Stuart."—D. O. Hill's painting.—T. Bell's poem.

THE author of the manuscript poem, "Antona's Banks"—written in 1797—has shewn how Fotheringhay Castle was the royal residence of the house of York:—

Lo! on that mound, in days of feudal pride,
Thy tow'ring castle frown'd above the tide;
Flung wide her gates, where troops of vassals met
With awe the brow of high Plantagenet.
But, ah! what chiefs in sable vests appear!
What bright achievements mark yon warrior's bier!
'Tis York's:—from Agincourt's victorious plain,
They bear the fallen hero o'er the main;
Through all the land his blooming laurels spread,
And to thy bosom give the mighty dead.
When from thy lap the ruthless Richard sprung,
A boding sound through all thy borders rung;
It spoke a tale of blood—fair Neville's woe,
York's murd'rous hand, and Edward's future foe.

The keep of the castle was built in the form of a fetter-lock, a circumstance which caused Philemon Holland, in his first edition of Camden's "Britannia," to "digress a little" into the following anecdote:—"Edmund of Langley, Duke of York, who built that keep, and garnished the glass windows there with fetter-locks, when he saw his sons, being younger scholars, gazing upon the painted windows, asked them what was the Latin for a fetter-lock. They, studying and looking silently one upon another, not able to answer, 'If you cannot tell me', says he, 'I will tell you. Hic hæc hoc taceatis, *i.e.*, hic hæc hoc—Be silent and quiet:' and therewithal added, 'God knoweth what may happen hereafter.' This, King Edward IV, his great-grandchild, publicly reported, when he, having attained the crown, created Richard, his younger son, Duke of York, and then commanding that he should use for his badge the *fetter-lock open*, to verify the presage of his great-grandfather." Up to that time, and while they were contending for the throne, the falcon was represented as endeavouring to expand its wings and force open the lock.

Passing underneath an avenue of limes that completely overarches the approach to the north porch of the church, let us ascend the belfrey-steps and climb up to the lantern, at whose lower story are the shattered figures of the four Evangelists standing upon embattled turrets. From this commanding station we have a bird's-eye view of Fotheringhay. Looking eastward, the village street cleaves past us to the left, having at its further extremity the picturesque New Inn, whose buildings form the three sides of a square, but whose inner galleries, existing when Nichols wrote his history, in

1787, have been since removed. We can see its Gothic gateway and flanking buttresses, and its mullioned windows, but three-fourths of this building, which once supplemented the accommodation afforded by the castle, has been converted into barns, and granaries, and farming purposes. Leading directly southward from this new Inn is the high road to Oundle, passing between an avenue of trees, and then crossing the Nene by the stone bridge which Queen Elizabeth had once repaired. Eastward from the New Inn we see a road leading into the fields and round to the castle ruins. Immediately to the right of this road, the grass-field on the other side of the hedge falls into a sweeping hollow, measuring seventy-five feet across, which we very clearly perceive to be the dried-up (and partially filled-up) bed of the outer moat. On the further side of its bank is a long wall, against the southern side of which barns and other farm-buildings have been erected. The further end of this is a genuine relic of the old castle, but I am sorry to miss, at this nearer end, a still more interesting relic, in the shape of the continuation of this wall, supported by three very massive buttresses, which were taken down by Lord Overstone (about the year 1863 or 1864), in order to use up their materials and gain a little space for some new farm-buildings. At the same time this portion of the outer moat was also filled up,

THE OUTER WALL AND MOAT, FOTHERINGHAY.

and has been converted into a garden. So far as I have been able to learn, no sketch of this outer-buttressed wall and moat is known to exist, save one that I myself took in 1852, and which I contributed to the volume for 1861 of the Amateur Anastatic Drawing Society.

And while on the subject of published illustrations of Fotheringhay Castle, I may here mention what is surely a very remarkable fact, when we consider the interest universally attaching to the spot, that only two representations of its remains have been published, viz., the frontispiece to Archdeacon Bonney's work (1821), and the print in Bridge's "Northamptonshire," which has been copied in several publications of Mr. Charles Knight. The latter view was taken in 1718, and shows Queen Elizabeth's bridge, and the river wall of the castle wherein two archways are discernible, beyond which is the Castle Mound. But of the appearance of the towers that rose from the mound, we have not the slightest record. No painting, engraving, or plan—not even the rudest scribble of the pen that could give us the least idea of the exterior or interior of any portion of Fotheringhay Castle—is known to exist. Books and manuscripts in the British Museum, the Bodleian, and other public and private libraries have been searched in vain, with the hope of meeting with some record, however rude and slight, of the ancient appearance of Fotheringhay Castle. Not even the Cottonian collection, despite the indefatigable industry of its founder, affords the most trivial help in this particular; and, although every other point in Mary's eventful history can be illustrated by contemporaneous engravings or paintings, yet, when we come to fatal Fotheringhay, there we encounter a total blank. It is as though the annihilation that visited the castle had also swept away every trace of it that had been made by the pencil or graver. Miss Strickland, the distinguished historian and biographer of Mary, Queen of Scots, possessed a Mary Stuart album, in which she had stored a goodly collection of drawings and prints to illustrate her favourite's life; but it lacked all records of Fotheringhay Castle, except those made in modern times.*

The late Mr. Joseph Cecil, of Northampton, a friend of the writer's, had a still more extensive collection (filling two enormous scrap-books), in which every spot (except Fotheringhay) that Mary ever visited is illustrated by contemporary views or plans, and every person with whom she ever had any dealings is represented by every known engraved portrait (sometimes forty in number), and by copies or photographs of portraits in oils. This collection is supposed to be unique, and was amassed by many years of intelligent labour and

* Including some by the writer. They are referred to in Miss Strickland's "Queens of Scotland," vii. 420, note.

valuable research regardless of cost, but it lacks any representation of Fotheringhay before its demolition. That no such record should be known to exist is certainly a curious fact.

I am glad to say that this unique collection of Mr. Cecil has now become national property, and has been added to the print-room at the British Museum. In the autumn of 1884, I happened to be in communication with Mr. Richard Sims, of the British Museum, on the subject of Fotheringhay. Mr. Sims had been applied to by the agent of a royal personage in Germany, who was desirous that Schiller's "Mary Stuart" * should be placed on the stage with as complete a scenic reproduction as was possible, of the localities introduced in the tragedy; and Mr. Sims wrote to me to help him with any details of Fotheringhay. This I did, assisted by Mr. Caparn, drawing-master of Oundle School; and the

* It was first produced at Weimar, in the year 1800. Racine had previously written a tragedy on the same theme. It was in his "Marie Stuart" that Rachel appeared; and a fine line engraving of this distinguished tragedienne—a full length portrait—costumed for the last scene in the Tragedy, will be found in "George Cruikshank's Omnibus: edited by Laman Blanchard," (Tilt and Bogue, 1842,) a magazine that numbered Thackeray among its contributors. The writer of the letterpress to the steel engraving of "Rachel, in the character of Marie Stuart," says, "Quiet, earnest, intense, with a look of passion that has its spring in tenderness, that is just the expression she should wear. It pervades all her performance, because in all of them she was the Woman. There it was, as you see it, when she said for this unhappy *Mary* that she was ready to go to death, for all that which could bind her to earth had passed away; and, as she said it, there came with its choking denial to her heart a sense of the still living capacity for joy or grief about to be quenched for ever." (p. 129.)

result was deemed highly satisfactory by Mr. Sims' royal patron. The arcade at Conington, and the window and staircase at Oundle, greatly helped to the scenic production of the banquet-hall.

I then mentioned to Mr. Sims the wish of Mrs. Cecil to carry out her late husband's desire that his Mary Stuart album should be added to the National collection. This was accomplished, early in 1885, after considerable correspondence with Professor Colvin; and it is a matter of thankfulness, that a collection so unique, and formed after years of labour, expense, and intelligent research, should now be preserved, where it is in safe custody and can be consulted by the artist and author. Previous to this, I have Mr. Sims' authority for saying, that, with the exception of the engravings already mentioned, the only illustrations of Fotheringhay in the National collection were two pencil sketches by Carter, the one representing the exterior of a building attached to the castle; and the other, a sketch of the ruins.

In this age of illustration and pictorial rendering of historical scenes, it also seems to me, somewhat surprising, that so interesting and picturesque a spot as Fotheringhay should not have been more frequently represented in engravings.

Pictures of Fotheringhay, too, are by no means frequent in our art exhibitions. I can recall but one, and that painted by a Scotsman, D. O. Hill, who treated the subject most poetically, with a twilight effect, taking his point of view from the opposite side of the river, and having the park-hill to the right, the castle mound in the centre, and the church to the left. When this picture was shown at the Edinburgh Exhibition, in 1852, it was thus described in a *brochure* entitled "Pictorial Musings":—

"He who seeks Nature in her gay attire,
Where streams smile back to heaven the bright sapphire,
When evening tints the azure vault with gold,
And zephyrs, 'mong the reeds, their wings enfold—
The soft sweet sunset of a summer day,—
May dream and ponder Hill's fair 'Fotheringhay.'"

In this picture a ghostly-looking heron, standing on the river's brink, was the only figure introduced. I looked upon the real scene on a twilight evening in the summer, and thought that it only wanted the solitary bird to realize the artist's picture, when flop! flop! a heron rose from the very spot amid the sedge upon the river's brink, and, wheeling into the air, bore away until he was lost in the sunset.

Mr. Thomas Bell, in his poem "On Fotheringhay Castle," shows how this portion of the quiet scenery and solitude of the Nene, may influence the imagination.

"Ah! what is that unearthly voice! Again
I hear its murmurs o'er the silent Nen;
It tells a tale of woe, of cruel hate,
Of England's shame, and Mary's ruthful fate!
Again I hear it, as it dies away,
Then louder swells, when gentle Zephyrs play,
And hov'ring o'er the hill, in accents clear,
Pours forth a mournful requiem on the ear
To Stuart's mem'ry, and to Stuart's fall;
Relates the horrors of the blood-stained hall,
Melvin's devotion, and the mournful train,
And fills the breast with sympathizing pain;
Till at the visionary scene I weep,
And o'er my senses chilling terrors creep."

Mr. Bell says, "Elizabeth's treatment of this accomplished Princess, her cousin, and a fugitive who sought her protection, must ever be considered as the foulest blot on the annals of her reign." An opinion which I heartily endorse.

CHAPTER VIII.

General view from the lantern of the Church.—Site of the Castle.—Robert Wyatt's find of Queen Mary's ring.—No ruins.—Queen Mary's rooms.—The moats.—The mill-brook.—The Mound.—Hawthorns.—The Scotch thistle.—Miss Strickland's opinion.—Wordsworth's Sonnet.—Burns' poem.

RETURNING from the artistic digression to our high position on the lantern of Fotheringhay Church, we see the castle mound, on which stood the keep and Mary's prison; and just beyond it the flat area on which was the fatal banqueting-hall, and the moat, and the various inequalities of the ground, with the hawthorn-trees scattered over them, and the shapeless fragment of the castle's masonry standing in solitary state near to the river; and, beyond the castle area, the line of hedge where flows the mill-brook which did duty for the outer moat; and then, the ground rising abruptly to the park hill, which has a high precipitous bank clothed with trees frowning over the river, which goes gleaming on with snake-like windings among the flat green meadows until it is well-nigh lost to view beneath the long timber viaduct of the Northampton and Peterborough Railway. The traveller who is journeying to the latter place by this railway should look out of the left-hand window shortly before he approaches Elton, and he will have an excellent view of Fotheringhay, with its church and castle-mound, at little more than half a mile distant. Beyond the railway-bridge we see the beautiful early-English spire of Warmington Church; and, further to the left, the tall tower of Elton Church, with the richly-timbered park of the Earl of Carysfort, and the high range of ground on the borders of Huntingdonshire.

Now let us descend from our high position to the village street, and, passing the Gothic portals of the New Inn, and the new farm-buildings that have replaced that old bit of buttressed wall, we walk by the side of the outer moat until we turn to the right, and find ourselves before the mound on which was the fetter-lock keep. A part of the moat is here filled up, and marks the former position of the drawbridge, the foundation of which was taken away in June, 1820, when a considerable portion of the foundation-stones of the castle were also removed. On this occasion the eastern side of the mound was dug into in the search for stone, and the excavations brought to light the back of a chimney, the entrances to two closets, and a pavement of Norman bricks. Some coins of Edwards II and IV were also found. One of the workmen employed on this occasion was a man of the name of Robert Wyatt, formerly a private in "The Prince of Wales's 3rd," who, having grown old, chiefly gained his living of late years by acting as guide to the castle ruins. He will doubtless be well remembered by many who read this book, to whom he will have told, as he has often told to the present writer, how he dug up the drawbridge, and how he filled-in the moat, and how a Scotch gentleman measured out the execution-room and found it correct, and, above all, how he himself had found Queen Mary's own ring. This was that signet-ring (with the inscription "Henri. L. Darnley, 1565," the monogram of Henry and Mary bound up in a true-lover's-knot, and the lion on a crowned shield within the hoop) of which Miss Strickland has given an illustration, and of which she says, "Perhaps it dropped from Mary's finger in her death agony on the block, and was swept away among the bloody sawdust unobserved." What a lucky find for the old man! I have searched again and again, year after year, in the ruins of Fotheringhay, but never found anything of greater consequence than some human bones that the rabbits had scratched out of a burrow on the eastern side of the mound. Robert Wyatt, then eighty-two years of age, and nearly blind, was enabled to tell his tale to Miss Strickland herself, and to Messrs. Parker, Freeman, and other learned antiquarians and members of the Archæological Society, when they visited Fotheringhay on Monday, July 29, 1861. "Miss Strickland proposed a subscription; and, the hat being sent round, the old man was made happy with a larger fee than his threadbare tales had probably ever won for him." This was, as it were, his last public appearance; for when I went to Fotheringhay early in September, 1862, my inquiries after Robert Wyatt were met by the painful information that, a short time previous, he had returned late in the evening from the Warmington "feast," considerably the worse for drink, and had been put to bed, and there found dead in the morning.

As soon as we have crossed the inner moat, and stand within the castle precincts, we plainly perceive that although there are no "ruins," in the accepted sense of the word, yet that abundant evidence is afforded by the moats, the artificial mound, the inequalities of the soil, and, above all, by the plentiful *débris* of stone, that a great building has once stood upon this spot. From the drawbridge, whose site we have just passed, a flight of stairs to the right anciently led to some "fair lodgings," and up higher to the wardrobe, and so on to the fetter-lock on the top of the mound, which enclosed about sixteen feet in the form of an octagon, with upper and lower chambers. Within the castle was a goodly court, leading to the spacious banqueting-hall, where the execution of Mary took place, and where also she was arraigned on her sham trial; and on the left hand was the chapel, some stately lodgings, and that "great dining-room, well garnished with pictures," which was mentioned in the survey of 1625. Miss Strickland is of opinion that "these were possibly the apartments appropriated to the use of the unfortunate Mary, where her last melancholy days were worn away." The foundations of the various outer and inner walls can be distinctly traced, and a ground-plan of the castle could be made with a probable approach to accuracy.

The inner moat, which is sixty-six feet wide, circles round the mount, which is everywhere precipitous, but more especially so on its northern and western sides. At these points the moat is thick with rushes, and still contains a little water, wherein the forget-me-not grows luxuriantly. On the other side the moat was the castle-yard, having, in its north-west corner, the great barn, a portion of which still remains. The inner moat ends by the river-front of the mount, which is about thirty-three yards distant from the Nene, which therefore served for the outer moat; but between the mount and the river there are traces of a wall, about twenty yards distant from the latter, and midway between this wall and the Nene is that shapeless block of masonry that is the sole representative of the castle architecture. The inner moat is continued from the drawbridge in an easterly direction, sweeping round the river. Though half-choked with reeds and rushes, yet it has not been filled up with earth; and its western bank, now fringed by fine hawthorns, is crowned with the stony *débris* of the brewhouses, bakehouses, and other adjuncts of the buttery and kitchen. Modern evidences of *al fresco* dinners may also be found in the tattered biscuit-bags littering the ground, and in the burnt patches where pic-nic parties have boiled their kettles.

On the other side of this moat is a flat grass field, about eighty yards in width, which was formerly the "yard half encompassing the castle," and which is bounded on its further or eastern side by the mill-brook flowing into the Nene, and forming the outer moat. This "yard" between the brook and the castle was laid out as an orchard and garden, and once contained a "great pond," which had been "landed up" when the survey was made in 1625. The mill-brook still flows in its former channel, rich in forget-me-nots, and shaded by hawthorns. A boat-house covers it at its junction with the river; and on the other side of it from the castle is "the little park," where the ground rises abruptly to a hill (its precipitous river-front clothed with foliage), from whence we have an excellent view of the castle precincts, the winding river, the beautiful church, and the village of Fotheringhay. About one hundred yards from the river the mill-

FOTHERINGHAY,
FROM THE OUTER MOAT,
WITH THE CASTLE MOUND.
Cuthbert Bede

brook is crossed by a well-made road-bridge of stone, coeval with the castle, having floodgates towards the river, the timbers of which are nearly destroyed from age. Here was the "gate-house, and another ruinous house," spoken of in 1625 survey; but, although they have disappeared, the interesting bridge still remains, and, with its adjuncts, will be found a capital subject for the artist, as well as the antiquarian.

The most conspicuous object in the sketches of the site of Fotheringhay Castle is the mound on which stood the fetterlock keep. At the present day its tenants are of a very peaceful and timid order, for it is completely honey-combed with rabbit-holes, whose indefatigable inhabitants are continually scratching up to the surface fragments of stone that, from their fresh colour, have evidently never seen daylight since the time of Edmund Langley. Fourteen hawthorns grow on various parts of the mound, many of them of great size and beauty; and scattered profusely over the mound, and the whole area of the castle, is Mary Stuart's own floral emblem —the Scotch thistle*—with its purple coronals, and its glossy

* "Few are the flowers that wave upon that mound;
No herb salubrious yields the blighted ground;
Beside the thorn the barren thistle springs:
The raven there his pilfer'd carrion brings
To glut in secret; or, impressed with fear,
Croaks his hoarse song to desolation's ear."
"Antona's Banks," (1797.)

green leaves veined with milky white, from which it has derived its name of the Milk Thistle *(Carduus marianus).* This is the thistle of which Tennyson speaks (in his Wellington Ode) :—

> "The stubborn thistle bursting
> Into glossy purples which out-redden
> The voluptuous garden rose."

But it has been a vexed question whether this or the cotton thistle *(Onopordium acanthium)* has the stronger claim to be called *the* Scotch thistle, and to figure as Scotia's emblem. The balance of testimony appears to lie in favour of the milk thistle; and certainly we are not inclined to dispute this decision here on the Fotheringhay mound, where, on this beautiful September morning, its purple blooms are charming the eye and awakening memories of the hapless "Queen of the Castle" (as Burleigh nicknamed her, when he wrote to Elizabeth a report of the sham trial in the banqueting-hall), who, doubtless, selected this milk thistle, from all others of its tribe, to be her national badge.

For, if this were not the case, how is it that we find this peculiar thistle (and not the cotton thistle) growing around and about all the prisons and palaces and castles from Dunbarton to Fotheringhay where Mary may have tarried? "Mary was a horticulturist and poet," says Miss Strickland, in a private letter to the writer of these lines; "and I should imagine that she sowed the seeds of the royal thistle of Scotland in the gardens of her English prisons." Or, if this may not have been the case at Fotheringhay, where, during the six winter months of her imprisonment she was confined to her bed or chamber, racked by neuralgic pains occasioned from loss of exercise and nineteen years' close detention in damp prisons, yet (as Miss Strickland further suggests) the appearance of this thistle at Fotheringhay and elsewhere, if not to be ascribed to Mary herself, may probably be attributed to the romantic gallantry of her many admirers, who wished the very ground to bring forth souvenirs of her whose presence had thrown a charm over the spot.

* * * * * * *

I append Wordsworth's Sonnet, supposed to have been written by Mary, Queen of Scots, in her "Captivity."*

"As the cold aspect of a sunless way
Strikes through the traveller's frame with deadlier chill,
Oft as appears a grove, or obvious hill,
Glistening with unparticipated ray,
Or shining slope where he must never stray;
So joys, remembered without wish or will,
Sharpen the keenest edge of present ill,—
On the crushed heart a heavier burthen lay.
Just Heaven, contract the compass of my mind
To fit proportion with my altered state!

* Poems of the Imagination. Miscellaneous Sonnets.

Quench those felicities whose light I find
Reflected in my bosom all too late!
Oh, be my spirit, like my thraldom, strait;
And, like mine eyes that stream with sorrow, blind!"

I may also here quote Burns' touching poem, the "Lament of Mary, Queen of Scots, on the approach of Spring." Burns thought highly of this poem; for, he wrote concerning it—"Whether it is that the story of our Mary, Queen of Scots, has a peculiar effect on the feelings of a poet, or whether I have, in the ballad, succeeded beyond my usual poetic success, I know not; but, it has pleased me beyond any effort of my muse for a good while past." I think that my readers will also be pleased to peruse it.

"Now Nature hangs her mantle green
On every blooming tree,
And spreads her sheets o' daisies white
Out owre the grassy lea:
Now Phœbus cheers the crystal stream,
And glads the azure skies;
But nought can glad the weary wight
That fast in durance lies.

Now lav'rocks wake the merry morn,
Aloft on dewy wing;
The merle, in his noontide bow'r,
Makes woodland echoes ring;
The mavis mild, wi' many a note,
Sings drowsy day to rest:
In love and freedom they rejoice,
Wi' care nor thrall opprest.

Now blooms the lily by the bank,
  The primrose down by the brae;
The hawthorn's budding in the glen,
  And milk-white is the slae;
The meanest hind in fair Scotland
  May rove their sweets amang;
But I, the Queen of a' Scotland,
  Maun lie in prison strang.

I was the Queen o' bonnie France,
  Where happy I hae been,
Fu' lightly rase I in the morn,
  As blythe lay down at e'en;
And I'm the sov'reign of Scotland,
  And mony a traitor there;
Yet here I lie in foreign bands,
  And never-ending care.

But, as for thee, thou false woman,
  My sister and my fae,
Grim vengeance, yet, shall whet a sword
  That thro' thy soul shall gae;
The weeping blood in woman's breast
  Was never known to thee;
Nor the balm that draps on wounds of woe
  Frae woman's pitying e'e.

My son! my son! may kinder stars
  Upon thy fortune shine;
And may those pleasure gild thy reign,
  That ne'er wad blink on mine!
God keep thee frae thy mother's faes,
  Or turn their hearts to thee;
And where thou meet'st thy mother's friend,
  Remember him for me!

Oh ! soon, to me, may summer suns
  Nae mair light up the morn !
Nae mair, to me, the autumn winds
  Wave o'er the yellow corn !
And in the narrow house o' death
  Let winter round me rave ;
And the next flow'rs that deck the spring,
  Bloom on my peaceful grave !

CHAPTER IX.

Mary brought to Fotheringhay.—Perio Lane.—Legends concerning it.—The Queen of Scots in prison.—Her rigorous treatment.—Insults offered her.—Queen Elizabeth's conduct.—A modern criticism.—Scenery of Fotheringhay.—Wordsworth's "Lament of Mary, Queen of Scots."

It was on the 25th of September, 1586, that Mary Queen of Scots was brought from Chartley to Fotheringhay by its castellan, Sir William Fitzwilliam (whose chivalrous kindness she acknowledged by bequeathing him that portrait of her son which hung at her bed's head at Fotheringhay, and which is still preserved by the family at Milton), by Sir Thomas Gorges, and by her rigorous gaoler, Sir Amyas Paulett. It is believed that she approached Fotheringhay by that south-western road which is called "Perry Lane"—the word being written "Perio," and twice so spelt on the Ordnance Map. At the corner of the lower end of this lane she would gain her first view of her last earthly home; the mound, then crowned with its castled towers, occupying the centre of the view, with the hill of the little park to the right, the church and village to the left, and the river winding at the foot of all, and spanned by her persecutor's bridge.

"The conviction," says Miss Strickland, in her History, "that her name was doomed to complete the melancholy list of princely sufferers whose calamities were associated with Fotheringhay Castle, elicited from Mary Stuart, on first beholding these gloomy towers from the lane or avenue of approach, which derives its name from that circumstance, the prophetic exclamation, '*Perio!*' I perish." And such is, indeed, the popular belief; but Miss Strickland told me, that, after she had quoted this legend in her History, she discovered a deed of a prior date to the time of Mary, Queen of Scots, in which the name "Perio" occurs. This, therefore, gives the finishing stroke to the old tradition in its present form, although it is quite possible that Mary Stuart may, when they entered upon Perio Lane, have been told its name, and then seized upon the idea contained in the word, and used it to express her own forebodings. Another legend is also attached to the word, which is thus given by Nichols: —"There is an idle tradition that Perry Mills, at a little distance from Fotheringhay, were so named from the queen's hearing a messenger's horn winding on that spot just before her execution, and thence expecting a reprieve; in her disappointment, she is said to have exclaimed, '*Perio!*'" Of a like complexion is the ridiculous couplet which says,

> "If Fotheringhay Castle had not been so nigh,
> Peterborough spires had not been so high!"

—a very hazy reference, I suppose, to her burial in Peterborough Cathedral. The above "idle tradition" is falsified by all the events of her execution.

The day of her death was February 8, 1587; and on the 19th of the previous December she had written her last noble letter to Elizabeth, never, either at that time or afterwards, expecting any better fate than the block, and only fearing that she might be privately murdered, and thus that her enemies might clear themselves by stigmatizing her memory with the sin of suicide. Those must have been six dismal wintry months that she passed at Fotheringhay, when the November fogs would settle heavily over the low-lying valley of the Nene, shrouding in their damp mystery the stretch of "dismal flats," and tending to aggravate her pensive melancholy and embitter her misery by adding to her severe bodily sufferings. Tortured with neuralgic pains, which so frequently kept her for days together to her bed, and crippled her from taking the least exercise, even if the weather and her goalers had permitted it, the wintry months of her detention at Fotheringhay must have been the most embittered of her many and long imprisonments. She could amuse her mind, it is true, by writing French verses; yet they were of this nature:—*

* Translated in Seward's "Anecdotes," ii. 155,

"Alas what am I? and in what estate?
    A wretched corse bereaved of its heart;
An empty shadow, lost, unfortunate:
    To die is now in life my only part.
Foes to my greatness! let your envy rest,
    In me no taste for grandeur now is found:
Consumed by grief, with heavy ills oppress'd,
    Your wishes and desires will soon be crown'd.
And you, my friends, who still have held me dear,
    Bethink you, that, when health and heart are fled,
    And every hope of fortune good is dead,
'Tis time to wish our sorrows ended here;
    And that this punishment on earth is giv'n
That I may rise to endless bliss in heav'n."

Three months before her death, her goaler insulted her by taking down the dais or canopy over her head, to signify to her that "she was a dead woman, and deprived of the honours and dignity of a queen;" and Paulett, covering his head in her presence, coarsely told her that as there was no longer any time or leisure for her to waste in idle recreations, he should take away her billiard-table; to which the Queen of Scots replied that she had never used it during those six weeks that she had been there; for that they had given her other occupations. So it was taken away from her, and not used again until its green cloth was torn off to form the first shroud for her headless corpse.

Her whole treatment at Fotheringhay was so rigorous

that it suggests the idea there was nothing her captors would have liked better than for Mary to have given them the chance of killing her. If she attempted to escape, she was to be shot by any of the two thousand soldiers that guarded her; if any attempted to rescue her, she was to be slain; if there was any noise or disturbance in her lodgings, or in the place where she was, she was to be at once put to death. Such were the standing orders during the time of her captivity at Fotheringhay; and these, combined with her well-grounded fear of secret assassination or poisoning, must have fearfully aggravated her sufferings, and have daily heaped fresh coals of fire on the head of Elizabeth. For the last two months of her imprisonment her chamber and bed were hung with black; and her forty-fourth and last birthday dawned upon her amid these funereal trappings.

I wonder if we shall ever know the real parts played by Elizabeth, Davison, Harrison, and Walsingham in that document of death which released the royal prisoner from all her indignities and sufferings? Partisanship, and conflicting considerations begotten of Roman Catholicism and Protestantism, unfortunately have so encrusted the subject, that, in gazing upon it, the clear eyes of the historian become dimmed, and more or less affected by those clouds of incense that Mary Stuart's worshippers have raised around her death and varied fortunes. The clue to Elizabeth's motives is one of those historical problems that admits of more than one solution.

I remember being present on an occasion when the instinct of a little workhouse girl guided her into the probable path for this discovery. It was at the examination of a certain industrial school of workhouse children, who, in a most surprising manner, answered questions that would infallibly have plucked many undergraduates and civil-service candidates. One of the examiners on this occasion was a member of Parliament, who had a good opportunity of airing his historical knowledge before the ladies and gentlemen who were present; and he at length asked the question, "What motives induced Queen Elizabeth to proceed to extreme measures against Mary, Queen of Scots?" "Because she was jealous of her," at once answered a bright-looking girl of fourteen, dressed in demure workhouse garb. The M. P. was scarcely satisfied with the answer; but, instead of resting content with it, he heedlessly asked, "And why was she jealous of her?" "Because Mary, Queen of Scots, was more beautiful and had more lovers!" was the prompt reply of Miss Workhouse. It is needless to say that the M.P. asked no more questions concerning Elizabeth and

Mary, Queen of Scots. It was time for him to close the subject; and it is time for me, also, to imitate his example.

Yet, ere we say farewell to Fotheringhay, stand with me here awhile on the mound on this lovely morning in the first week of September, when all around looks so sweetly calm and peaceful that it is hard to realize the fact that, this spot was devoted to the consummation of a wicked deed that (happily) stands alone in our historic annals. Nor, just now, can we realize those November fogs and wintry mists that must have made the prospect so cheerless to the royal captive's eyes; for, bathed in the brightness of a meridian sun, the landscape borrows a beauty that is not its own, and would be accounted sufficiently picturesque to meet the tastes of all who, like truth-speaking Goldsmith, preferred a flat country where you could walk about without fatigue, to a highland district where precipitous mountains gave the pedestrian unnecessary toil. Yet the flatness of the greater portion of the landscape is relieved by the extensive woods and gentle hills that bound the view; and the level stretch of meadows immediately before us is girdled by the shining windings of the river, and dappled over with flocks and herds. Down by the water's edge, standing knee-deep in the cooling stream, and whisking the summer flies with busy tails, a bevy of cows have pushed their way through the sedgy margin of the river, and are mirrored in its clear surface, where the fishes are rising, and making white circles in the dusky shadows of the bank. Other evidences of a peaceful agricultural life meet the eye, in rick-yards and homesteads, and in those English gold-fields where the white-shirted reapers are making paths through the golden grain, while the heavy-laden waggons bear away their rich freight of treasure. Nearer still, the sun gleams on the ruddy hawthorn-berries on the castle mound, on the turquoise patches of the bright forget-me-nots in the sedgy moat, and on the glossy purples of the chosen flower of the Queen of Scots.

It is a scene of peace, gazing on which we think of her own words, "That soul is far unworthy of the joys of heaven whose body cannot endure for a moment the stroke of the executioner."

* * * * * * *

Here—before I append an account of the mock trial and ghastly execution, I may aptly quote from Wordsworth's beautiful poem, the "Lament of Mary, Queen of Scots, on the Eve of a New Year"—her last New-year's eve upon earth being destined to be spent amid funereal trappings in her gloomy prison at Fotheringhay.

"Smile of the moon!—for so I name
That silent greeting from above;
A gentle flash of light that came
From her whom drooping captives love;
Or art thou of still higher birth?
Thou that didst part the clouds of earth,
My torpor to reprove!

Bright boon of pitying Heaven—alas!
I may not trust thy placid cheer!
Pondering that time to-night will pass
The threshold of another year;
For years to me are sad and dull;
My very moments are too full
Of hopelessness and fear.

And yet, the soul-awakening gleam,
That struck perchance the farthest cone
Of Scotland's rocky wilds, did seem
To visit me, and me alone;
Me, unapproached by any friend,
Save those who to my sorrows lend
Tears due unto their own.

To-night, the church-tower bells will ring
Through these wide realms a festive peal;
To the new year a welcoming;
A tuneful offering for the weal
Of happy millions lulled in sleep;
While I am forced to watch and weep,
By wounds that may not heal.

Born all too high, by wedlock raised
Still higher—to be cast thus low!
Would that mine eyes had never gazed
On aught of more ambitious show
Than the sweet flowerets of the fields!
It is my royal state that yields
This bitterness of woe.

Yet how?—for I, if there be truth
In the world's voice, was passing fair;
And beauty, for confiding youth,
Those shocks of passion can prepare
That kill the bloom before its time,
And blanch, without the owner's crime,
The most resplendent hair.

Unblest distinction! showered on me
To bind a lingering life in chains:—
All that could quit my grasp, or flee,
Is gone;—but not the subtle stains
Fixed in the spirit; for even here
Can I be proud that jealous fear
Of what I was remains.

A woman rules my prison's key;
A sister Queen, against the bent
Of law and holiest sympathy,
Detains me, doubtful of the event;
Great God, who feel'st for my distress,
My thoughts are all that I possess,
Oh, keep them innocent!

Farewell desire of human aid,
Which abject mortals vainly court,
By friends deceived, by foes betrayed,
Of fears the prey, of hopes the sport;
Nought but the world-redeeming cross
Is able to supply my loss,
My burthen to support.

Hark ! the death-note of the year
Sounded by the castle clock !
From her sunk eyes a stagnant tear
Stole forth, unsettled by the shock ;
But oft the woods renewed their green,
Ere the tired head of Scotland's queen
Reposed upon the block !"*

* This poem was penned in 1817, and will be found in Wordsworth's "Poems founded on the Affections."

PART II.

Historical.

A BRIEF HISTORY OF THE TRIAL AND EXECUTION OF MARY, QUEEN OF SCOTS, AT FOTHERINGHAY CASTLE.

PART I.—THE MOCK TRIAL.

In less than three weeks after the Queen of Scots' removal from Chartley to Fotheringhay, the thirty-four out of the forty-six Peers appointed by Queen Elizabeth* as a Commission for her trial, assembled at Fotheringhay, on October 11th. 1586 (the 21st of October by modern reckoning), and had to be accommodated at the New Inn and various houses

* "After delivering the deed to her secretary, Davison, and commending him to carry it to the Chancellor, she affected to have changed her mind; and burst forth in lamentations, when informed that it had passed into the hands of those whose duty it was to see that the Queen's mandate was obeyed. Never was a piece of acting more clumsily performed, because no one was deceived by it. Elizabeth intended from the first that Mary should die; and her sole regret was, that there should not be found among her loving subjects, persons willing to sacrifice both honour and life, in order that her character might be screened from the ignominy of participating in the execution."

"*History of England*," *by Rev. George R. Gleig, M.A.*

in the village, the precincts of the castle being already filled with the two thousand soldiers and others who had already been quartered there.

The Queen of Scots was confined to her bed by indisposition; but Sir Amyas Paulet introduced to her presence Sir Walter Mildmay, Chancellor of the Exchequer, and Barker, the Notary, who gave her the letter in which Queen Elizabeth declared to her that her crimes were discovered,—that she was amenable to the laws of England, and that the Commissioners had been sent to hear, and enquire into, the cause.

Mary replied that she was sorry that her good sister, the Queen, had refused the offers made in her behalf: that she had nearly lost the use of her limbs through her long captivity; that she was innocent of any plot against the Queen of England, and that she herself was a Queen, and would not prejudice the son who was to succeed her, by behaving as though she were a subject: that she had been deprived of all her papers, and was ignorant of the laws of the country; and that she was willing to refer any controversy to the judgment of foreign princes.

They retired from her presence, but again waited upon her to read over to her what she had stated to them, and to enquire if she adhered to those statements. She replied in the affirmative; but wished to add, that she had not lived under the protection of the law; but, that when she came to crave it, the Queen had put her in prison.

Lord Chancellor Bromley, accompanied by Burghley, Hatton, and others, then waited upon her, advising her to appear at her trial, or that they would proceed with it in her absence. Mary replied that she would rather die a thousand deaths before she would acknowledge herself as a subject; and that she would answer only before a free and full Parliament. As for the Commission, she did not know how it was composed; and, very probably, they had already condemned her; but, she would have them "to look into their consciences, and to remember that the theatre of the world was wider than the realm of England." Burghley then changed his tactics, and sought to win her consent; wherein he was supported by Sir Christopher Hatton; and, though, for some time, she declared that she would only appear before the Queen in Council, or the Estates of the realm lawfully assembled, she finally consented to appear, if her protest against the competency of the tribunal was placed on record.

On the next morning, Friday, October 14th, at nine o'clock, Mary, walking with difficulty, from rheumatism, and supported on either side by Burgoigne, her physician, and Sir Andrew Melville, Master of the Household, descended to the great hall of the castle,* where benches were placed against the walls for the Commissioners, the Earls on one side, and the Barons on the other. Dressed in black velvet,† with a white lawn veil thrown over her pointed widow's cap, with one of her ladies bearing her train, and three other of her ladies following her, she took her seat on a chair in the centre of the hall, a footstool being placed for her feet. Looking at the chair of state raised at the upper end of the hall for the Queen of England, she proudly said, "I am a Queen by birth, and have been the Consort of a King of France; my place should have been there." Bowing gracefully to the nobles, she said to Sir Andrew Melville, "Alas! how many counsellors! and not one for me."

The trial was then opened by Lord Chancellor Bromley, who said that the Queen of England having been acquainted with Mary's plot against her person, her realm and her religion, desired to know, through her Commissioners, whether she pleaded guilty or not guilty to the charge.

Although suffering from rheumatism, she rose and addressed the Commissioners, reminding them that she had

* A fine painting, by Mr. Laslett J. Pott, of "Mary, Queen of Scots, descending the steps of the hall at Fotheringhay," is to be seen in the famous gallery of pictures formed by Mr. A. G. Kurtz, at Grove House, Wavertree, Liverpool, and generously thrown open by him to the public.

† Froude says she wore "a plain grey dress": but this is not borne out by other historians.

come to England to seek the assistance that had been promised to her by a Queen, who had thrown her into prison, but who had no jurisdiction over her; and that she had appeared there, solely to protest against the unfounded charges made against her, and which she was ready to hear and refute, although she did not consider any of those present to be her peers or judges.

Gawdy, the Queen's Serjeant, then opened the case for the Crown detailing the circumstances of the Babington conspiracy, and reading the three letters purporting to have been sent to him by Mary, on which the charge against her depended. These documents were copies and not the originals; and she denied that she had written them. As to the letter in cipher, which was said to be hers, she said that it was easy to imitate ciphers; and she implied that Walsingham might have had something to do with it. He indignantly denied this; upon which she begged him not to be displeased with her, and would forgive her if she had accused him wrongfully, and that he should do the same to her. "Spies" she said, "are men of doubtful credit, who make a show of one thing and speak another; therefore, I beseech you not to believe that I have ever consented to the Queen's, my sister's, destruction. I would not make shipwreck of my soul by conspiring her destruction."

The Commissioners replied that witnesses would be called; and they then adjourned for an interval.

On reassembling, more letters were brought forward, that were alleged to have been written by Babington, and her secretaries, Nau and Curle. She demanded that if there were any letters in her own hand-writing, they should be produced; that if anything hurtful to the Queen had been written by them, it was done without her knowledge; and that she ought not to be convicted except by her own words and writing. "I am held in chains:" she said. "I have no counsel, you have deprived me of my papers, and all means of preparing my defence, which must, therefore, be confined to a solemn denial of the crime imputed to me; and I protest, on the sacred honour of a Queen, that I am innocent of practising against your Sovereign's life. I do not, indeed, deny that I have longed for liberty, and earnestly laboured to procure it. Nature impelled me to do so; but, I call God to witness that I have never conspired the death of the Queen of England. I have written to my friends, and solicited them to assist me to escape from her miserable prisons, in which she has kept me now nearly nineteen years, till my health and hopes have been cruelly destroyed; but I never wrote the letters you pretend, nor would I have done so, to purchase a crown. I cannot answer, indeed, that my secretaries may not have received and answered such letters; but, if so, it was unknown to me, and I claim the privilege of being convicted on my own writing alone, or words proved by lawful witnesses; but, sure I am, nothing of the kind can be produced against me."

Burghley, after accusing her of complicity in the criminal designs of Morgan, Paget and Mendoza, to which Mary replied with the same vigour and decision, without falling into any of the traps so astutely laid for her, the proceedings of the first day of the trial were brought to a close.

On the following morning, the Queen of Scots again appeared in the hall, attended as on the preceding day; but the Attorney and Solicitor General and Queen's Serjeant took no part in the proceedings, which were conducted by Burghley, who brow-beat her "with great stomaching"—as he himself expressed it in a letter to Davison. He endeavoured to confuse her by touching upon a variety of topics apart from the main issue, to which she had repeatedly to bring him back; but he would not reply to her demands to be confronted with her secretaries, and to produce the letters that were attributed to her. "My innocence," she said, "is well known to God. My crimes consist in my birth, the injuries that have been inflicted on me, and my religion. Of the first, I am justly proud; the second I can forgive; and the third has been my sole consolation and hope under all my afflictions; and, for its advancement, I would cheerfully give my best blood, if so be I might, by my own death, procure relief for the suffering Catholics. But, not even for their sakes would I purchase it at the price of the blood of others, having always been tender of the lives of the meanest of God's creatures. It is, in sooth, more in accordance with my nature to pray with Esther, than to play the part of Judith. I know you call me irreligious. There was, indeed, a time when I would willingly have been instructed in the Protestant creed; but, that was not permitted, my soul being regarded of no value." Here she wept bitterly: but the assembled commissioners

"Saw fair Mary weep in vain."*

"Look here, my lords," she said, drawing a ring from her finger. "I came to England relying upon the friendship and promises of your Queen. Look at this pledge of love and protection that I received from your mistress. Regard it well. Trusting to this pledge I came among you. You all know how it has been kept." This was the diamond ring that Elizabeth had sent to her when she was a prisoner at Lochleven, with the assurance, that, if she could effect her escape, the English Queen would meet her on the border

* Sir Walter Scott's ballad of "Cadzow Castle."

with a force sufficient to protect her against her rebellious subjects.

Mary was then charged with corresponding with Mendoza and offering to make over the kingdom of England to the King of Spain; and she complained bitterly that her letters had been garbled, and perverted to meanings that they did not bear. Burghley plodded on, labouriously, with the evidence that had been laid before the commissioners; and acquitted himself so much to his own satisfaction, that, in his letter to Davison, he boasted of the skill and success with which he had encountered and defeated "The Queen of the Castle," as he nicknamed the Queen of Scots. "My lord," she said, "you are my enemy." "I am the enemy," he replied, "of all Queen Elizabeth's adversaries." Mary demanded to have an advocate, and another day to prepare her defence. And, when Burghley refused this, she rose with scorn, and left the hall, demanding to be heard in a full Parliament in presence of the Queen of England and her Council.

The Court then abruptly broke up at one o'clock, and the so-called Trial was ended. For two days, the Queen of Scots had stood at bay against thirty-six assailants, displaying the courage and ability that were her great characteristics. Her life now lay at the mercy of Elizabeth.

In speaking of this trial, Sir James Mackintosh says, "It is impossible to read without admiration, in the minute records of the trial, the self-possessed, prompt, clear, and sagacious replies by which the forlorn woman defended herself against the most expert lawyers and politicians of the age, who, instead of examining her as judges, pressed her with the unscrupulous ingenuity of enemies."

Mr. John Hosack, in his "Mary, Queen of Scots and her Accusers," says of this trial, "It cannot be denied that, even according to their own account, and we have no other, she had maintained throughout a decisive superiority over her opponents. Without counsel, or witnesses, or papers, and armed with nothing but her own clear intellect and heroic spirit, she had answered, point by point, all their allegations."

Froude says, "She had confidence in her presence of mind, in her intellect, in the majesty of her appearance and bearing. She had never yet, in private, encountered any man, except perhaps John Knox, who had resisted wholly the fascination of her presence. The first lawyers in England would be in the court, but on that score she had neither diffidence nor alarm. She was not afraid to encounter the ablest of them with their special weapon of the tongue, and she had no fear that they would have the advantage of her. * * * She perfectly comprehended Elizabeth's character. The court had been commissioned to pass sentence."

Dr. Lingard says, "She was placed in a situation in which, though she might assert, it was impossible that she could prove her innocence. A single and friendless female, the inmate of a prison for the last nineteen years, ignorant of the law, unpractised in judicial forms, without papers, or witnesses, or counsel, and with no other knowledge of the transactions than the reports collected by her female servants, nor of the proofs to be adduced by her adversaries but what her conjectures might supply. She could be no match for that array of lawyers, judges and statesmen, who sat marshalled against her; and if, among the commissioners, she espied two or three secret friends, they were men whose fidelity was suspected, and whose lives and fortunes probably depended on their vote of that day; the rest comprised the most distinguished of those who, for years, had sought her death in the council, or had clamourously called for it in Parliament. Yet, under all these disadvantages she defended herself with spirit and address. For two days she kept at bay the hunters of her life; on the third, the proceedings were suspended by an adjournment to Westminster."

Sir Walter Scott says, "Mary, left to herself, and having counsel of no friend, advocate, or lawyer, made, nevertheless, a defence becoming her high birth and distinguished talents. * * * Through the whole sitting of the court, unaided by counsel or legal advice of any kind, she sustained and repelled the accusations brought against her by professional persons of eminence, with an ingenuity and address which could hardly have been expected from a person of her rank, sex and education."

PART II.—AFTER THE TRIAL.

MARY kept her bed for some days after this mock trial, and the departure of the commissioners, who met again, on the 25th of October, in the Star Chamber at Westminster. The two secretaries, Nau and Curle, were examined; and the former affirmed that the principal heads of accusation—those alone on which could be based any pretext of condemnation—were false. His testimony was not accepted; and sentence of death—at the pleasure of the Queen—was pronounced against the two secretaries and Mary, Queen of Scots. A clause was added, that this judgment would not affect her son's claim to the throne.

The sentence of the commissioners was brought before the Lords and Commons who besought the Queen to put it in immediate execution. To which request, Elizabeth made this ambiguous reply,—"If I should say that I meant not to grant your petition, by my faith, I should say unto you more perhaps than I mean. And if I should say that I mean to grant it, I should tell you more than is fit for you to know. Thus, I must deliver to you an answer answerless."

Elizabeth bade her kinsman, the accomplished young

nobleman, Lord Buckhurst, (author of the tragedy "Porrex and Ferrex,") to go to Fotheringhay and communicate the sentence of death to Mary, Queen of Scots. Beale, the Clerk of the Council, went with him, and they reached Fotheringhay on the 19th of November. They executed their commission, the royal prisoner, who was still ill, receiving the tidings with great fortitude. On the day of their departure, Sir Amyas Paulet—with whom Sir Drue Drury was now associated as keeper of the Queen's person—insulted Mary by knocking down the dais, covering his head in her presence, and saying that he should take away her billiard-table, as she had no longer time or leisure to waste on idle recreations. To which she replied, that she had never used the table, as they had given her other occupations.

Mary then wrote to Elizabeth, thanking God, that it had pleased Him, through her, to put an end to the wearisome pilgrimage of her life. She asked nothing for herself, except that her body, after death, might be given over to her servants to be buried in France, where it might find that repose, which, living, it had never known. She begged also that she might not be put to death in secret, but in the presence of her servants and others, who might testify that she died in the true faith. And she further prayed that her servants might be allowed to go freely where they pleased.

She begged Elizabeth to give her a word in her own hand, to say that she would grant these requests. But, the Queen never replied to the letter, although, in writing to Walsingham, she said, "There is a letter from the Scottish Queen that hath wrought tears, but I trust shall do no further harm, albeit the delay is too dangerous."

On the plea that a new plot against the Queen's life had been discovered, the sentence of death against the Queen of Scots, was publicly proclaimed by heralds, with the sound of trumpets, on the fourth of December, and was received in London,* and all through the country, with frantic delight, the ringing of church bells and the blazing of bonfires.

Through the intervention and remonstrances of the French King, the Queen of Scots life was spared for a time, though she was in daily expectation of secret assassination. A deputation had waited upon her at Fotheringhay, announcing the sentence that had been pronounced upon her in London: and on her forty-fifth birthday, the 11th of December,† the royal prisoner found that her bed and chamber were hung

* In Dr. Freshfield's privately printed book of the Registers of St. Christopher-le-Stocks, in the City of London, is the following: "Item, paide for ringing when Babington with thother traytors were apprehended and weare takenn, and also when the queen of scotts was behedded." The last word has been struck through with a pen, and the words "proclamed conspirator to ye queen and our realme" substituted.

† The date is somewhat uncertain. The 8th, 11th, and 12th being variously given.

with black, to intimate that she was to be regarded as a dead woman. Sir Amyas Paulet wrote to Walsingham that he feared "Fotheringhay was forgotten, although the lady under his charge had given all her Majesty's true and faithful subjects cause not to sleep soundly till the head and seed-plot of all practises and conspiracies were utterly extirpated;" while Queen Elizabeth was often heard to lament that among the many who professed to be attached to her, not one would spare her the necessity of dipping her hands in the blood of a sister Queen. Both Sir Amyas Paulet and Sir Drue Drury refused to make shipwreck of their conscience by shedding blood without law or warrant.

While the Queen of England kept Christmas with her Court at Greenwich, the Queen of Scots was languishing in her prison at Fotheringhay, in hourly anticipation of death and racked with rheumatic pains, increased by the dense fogs and mists that arose from the flat meadows by the river. In the middle of January, Sir Andrew Melville, the Master of the Household, was removed from the Castle; and, on the night of Sunday, January 29th, the soldiers who were on guard under the prison window were alarmed by the appearance of a brilliant meteor, which appeared thrice just before her window.

Two days after this, Elizabeth signed, at Greenwich, the

order for the execution of the Queen of Scots, saying that it was made needful, and desiring to be troubled no further on the subject till all was over, but suggesting the hall of the Castle as a fitter place than the court-yard for the scene of the execution. Secretary Beale, in company with the executioner—who was clad in a suit of black velvet,—arrived at Fotheringhay, on Sunday, February the fifth. Early the next day, Beale went in search of Lord Shrewsbury, who was staying in the neighbourhood, and sent a messenger to the Sheriff of Northamptonshire to be in attendance at the Castle on Wednesday morning. The Earl of Kent got to Fotheringhay on Monday, and the Earl of Shrewsbury on the following day, when they demanded an audience of the Queen of Scots, who was in bed, suffering from a rheumatic attack. She, however, rose, and received them, sitting in a chair at the foot of the bed.

In the presence of these two Lords, with Paulet, Drury, Beale, and her attendants, the warrant of her execution was read by Beale. She listened to it attentively and with composure, thanking God for the tidings that the end of her troubles was at hand. "I did not think," she said, "that the Queen, my sister, would ever have consented to my death; but, God's will be done. He is my principal witness, that I shall render up my spirit into His hands innocent of any offence against her, and with a pure heart and conscience clear before His divine majesty of the crimes whereof I am accused. That soul is far unworthy of the joys of Heaven, whose body cannot endure for a moment the stroke of the executioner."

Mr. Froude says that "she was dreadfully agitated" and that "she broke down altogether." But, this is not in accordance with all the contemporary accounts of Camden, Jebb, Egerton and others; and Burghley's reporter wrote thus to his patron—"She seemed not to be in any terror, for aught that appeared by her outward gesture or behaviour; but rather, with smiling cheer and pleasing countenance, digested and accepted the said admonition of preparation to her unexpected execution, saying that her death would be welcome to her." This behaviour accords with her whole conduct during the last scenes of her life.

She enquired as to the date of her execution; when Lord Shrewsbury replied, "To-morrow morning, at eight o'clock." "That is very sudden, and leaves no time for preparation," she said; and she asked for time to make her will and put her affairs in order. Beale said that she had already had two months to prepare for her fate: and Lord Shrewsbury told her the execution could not be deferred. Lord Kent said that she might have the Bishop or Dean of Peterborough for her consolation; and recommended her to choose the Dean, who was a learned divine who would "be able to show her the errors of her false religion." She firmly replied that she would die in her faith and would willingly shed her blood in its cause. The Earl of Kent said "Your life would be the death of your religion, and your death will be its preservation." "I did not flatter myself," she replied, "that I was worthy of such a death, and I humbly receive it as an earnest of my acceptance into the number of God's chosen servants."

She then spoke of those who had intrigued against her, and had detained her in cruel captivity for nineteen years. Placing her hand on a New Testament, she said, "I take God to witness, that I never desired, sought, nor consented to the death of your Queen." The Earl of Kent said "That book is a Popish Testament; and an oath taken on that Testament is as worthless as the book itself." She replied, "It is, according to my belief, the true Testament. Would you, my lord, give more credit to my oath, if I swore upon your version, which I do not believe?" She then enquired if her son had forgotten his mother in her distress; and whether any foreign powers had interceded in her behalf. The Earl of Shrewsbury, with the others, then withdrew, after he had given the Queen of Scots into the custody of Sir Amyas Paulet.

Burgoigne and her other servants gave way to their distress, when Mary said to Jane Kennedy, "Up! leave weeping and be doing, for the time is short. Did I not tell you that it would come to this? Blessed be God that it has come, and that fear and sorrow are at an end. Weep not, for it will avail nothing: but, rejoice that you see me so near the end of my long troubles and afflictions. Now, then, take it patiently, and let us pray God together." She then prayed with them; after which she divided her money into portions, putting each portion into a little purse, with instructions to whom it should be given.

After supper, she pledged them in a cup of wine—the cup being made of an Indian nut, mounted in silver. She bequeathed it to her god-daughter, Mary Strickland, of Sizergh Castle, Westmoreland; and it is still preserved. She then divided her wardrobe and jewels among her women; sending her sapphire ring to her kinsman, Lord Claud Hamilton. She then wrote to De Préan, her almoner, who was housed in the castle, but denied admittance to her, praying him that he would keep vigil that night, and that as she was denied receiving the Sacrament, she must content herself with a general confession. Perhaps, in the morning, when she was brought forth, she might see him and ask for his blessing on her knees.

She then, with much celerity, made her will, writing it on two sheets of paper. She also wrote a letter to the King of France; but, being exhausted, she said she would take some repose, after her damsels had washed her feet. Jane Kennedy read, at her request, from the Book of Hours, the story of the penitent thief. "He was a great sinner," she said, "but not so great a sinner as I am. May my blessed Saviour, in memory of His passion, have mercy on me in the hour of death, as He had upon him."

She then lay down on her bed for the last time, while her faithful maidens kept watch by her bedside. They saw that her eyes were closed, but her lips moved as if in prayer.

And thus, the Queen of Scots spent her last night on earth.

PART III.—THE EXECUTION.

The morning of the Execution came—Wednesday, the 8th of February, 1587; but, before it had dawned, the Queen of Scots had risen from her bed, and, at six o'clock, her ladies, at her own request, had dressed her "as for a festival," as "she had but two hours to live."

Her dress, according to the contemporary account sent to Lord Burghley, was as follows:—"On her head she had a dressing of lawn, edged with bone lace, a pomander chain, and an Agnus Dei about her neck, a crucifix in her hand, a pair of beads at her girdle, with a golden cross at the end of them, a veil of lawn fastened to her cowl, bowed out with wire, and edged round about with bone lace; her gown was of black satin, printed, with a train and long sleeves to the ground, set with acorn buttons of jet and trimmed with pearl, and short sleeves of black satin, cut, with a pair of sleeves of velvet whole under them; her kirtle wholly of a figured black satin, and her petticoat upper-body, unlaced in the back, of crimson satin, and her petticoat skirt of crimson velvet; her shoes of Spanish leather, with the rough side outwards, a pair of green silk garters, her nether stockings worsted coloured watchet, clocked with silver, and next her legs a pair of Jersey hose, white."

Miss Agnes Strickland, quoting from a contemporary manuscript in the Vatican, written by an eye-witness of the execution, says that "she had caused a camisole of fine Scotch plaid, reaching from the throat to the waist, but without a collar, to be prepared the night before, that, when her upper garments should be removed, she might escape the distress of appearing uncovered before so many people."

She then prayed earnestly in her oratory, her devotions including the following prayer:—

"O Domine Deus! speravi in Te;
O care me Jesu, nunc libera me!
In durâ catena, in miserâ pœna, desidero Te!
Languendo, gemendo, et genuflectendo,
Adoro, imploro, ut liberes me!"

"My Lord and my God, I have hoped in Thee;
O Jesu, sweet Saviour, now liberate me.
I have languished for Thee in affliction and chains;
Lamenting and sighing through long years of pains.
Adoring, imploring, on humbly bowed knee,
I crave, of Thy mercy, by grace set me free." *

---

* Another paraphrase of Queen Mary's prayer is as follows, and has been set to music by Dr. Harington, of Bath:—

"In this last solemn and tremendous hour,
My Lord, my Saviour, I invoke Thy pow'r!
In these sad pangs of anguish and of death,
Receive, O Lord, Thy suppliant's parting breath!

After her private devotion, she concluded her letter to her brother-in-law, Henry III, King of France, signing it, "The morning of my death, this Wednesday, 8th February. Marie R." She then returned to her bed-chamber, where, sitting by the fire, she consoled her attendants. Bourgoigne then brought her a little wine and a piece of toasted bread, which he begged her to take: and she, smilingly, thanked him for bringing her her last meal, and begged him to read her will before her servants. This he did; and she then asked them all to kneel down and pray with her for the last time.

While they were thus engaged, the castle clock struck the hour of eight, and Thomas Andrews, the High Sheriff, rapped at the door of the ante-chamber, to command her attendance. Being told that she was engaged in prayer, he left her for a quarter of an hour; and then, returning with Sir Amyas Paulet, the Earls of Shrewsbury and Kent, Beale, and several others, he was admitted to the room, at the upper end of which, Mary and her attendants were still kneeling.

"Madam," he said, in a faltering voice, "the Lords have sent me for you." "Yes! let us go!" she replied: and

---

Before Thy hallow'd cross she prostrate lies,
O hear her prayers, commiserate her sighs!
Extend Thy arms of mercy and of love,
And bear her to Thy peaceful realms above!"

Burgoigne assisted her to rise. As her own faithful servants would not lead her to death, she asked for the assistance of two of Sir Amyas Paulet's servants, who led her from the room. The two Earls prevented the ladies and attendants from following her: and Mary entreated them to allow her "poor afflicted servants to be with her at her death, that they might see how patiently their Queen endured it." With inconceivable brutality the Earl of Kent replied that her request could not be granted, as they might be troublesome by their speeches and behaviour, and also "would not stick to put some superstitious trumpery in practise, if it were but dipping their handkerchiefs in her blood."

"My lord," said Mary, "I will pass my word they do no such thing. Alas! poor souls, it will do them good to bid their mistress farewell. Your mistress, being a maiden queen, for womanhood's sake, would not deny me this courtesy. I know she hath not so straitened your commission but that you might grant me more than this, if I were of a far meaner condition."

Seeing they would not grant her request, she added, with tears, "I am cousin to your Queen! descended of the blood-royal of Henry VII; a married Queen of France, and the anointed Queen of Scotland."

After a consultation, they reluctantly granted her request

in part, and permitted that two of her women and four of her men should attend her. She selected Jane Kennedy and Elizabeth Curle,* who had always slept in her bed-room, and had been with her for upwards of twenty years,—Sir Andrew Melville, Master of the Household; Bourgoigne, her physician; Gourion, her surgeon; and Gervais, her apothecary. Then she bade a tender farewell to the others, who were locked in the room; but whose cries penetrated even to the banquet-hall.

She then lent on the arms of Paulet's two retainers, saying, with pleasant courtesy, "it is the last trouble that I shall give you." At the foot of the great staircase, Melville flung himself on his knees before her in great grief that it should be his lot to carry back to Scotland such sad tidings.

"Melville," she said, "you should rather rejoice than weep that the end of Mary Stuart's troubles is come. Tell my friends I die a true Catholic. Commend me to my son; tell him I have done nothing to prejudice his kingdom of Scotland. So, good Melville, farewell." And she stooped and kissed her faithful old servant on the cheek. She then asked for her chaplain, but he had been refused admission.

Sir William Fitzwilliam, of Milton, who then held Fother-

* Dr. Lingard calls her "Elspeth" Curle. Froude erroneously says, "Elizabeth Kennedy and Curle's young wife, Barbara Mowbray."

inghay on a lease from the Crown, stepped forward to kiss her hand, and to express "his regret and indignation that her blood should be cruelly shed while under his roof." Mary thanked him for "his gentle entertainment of her, and begged that he would accept as a memorial of her grateful appreciation of his courtesy, the picture of the King, her son, which was hanging at her bed's head, and which was the last remaining possession she had not bequeathed."

Then the procession passed into the banquet-hall, cleared of its tables and forms, Andrews, the High Sheriff, being first, followed by Sir Amyas Paulet and Sir Drue Drury—the Earl of Kent—Beale—and the Earl of Shrewsbury with his marshal's baton. The Queen of Scots, her train borne by Melville, and followed by her attendants, entered the hall with a firm step and unruffled composure, though, for the first time, she was in sight of the scaffold. It was erected at the upper end of the hall, near to the large fire-place, in which a fire was burning. It was a platform, twelve feet square, two and a half high, covered with black cloth, as were the rails that surrounded it. On the platform was the block, covered with black, the axe, a chair covered with black, with a square black velvet cushion before it, and two stools for the two Earls. The scaffold was surrounded by a strong guard of halberdiers, and Earl Marshal's men, nearly two hundred in number; and about a hundred gentlemen of the neighbourhood were in the hall. Outside, in the court-yard, were many hundreds, who, while waiting for the completion of the execution, were entertained with music.*

There were two steep steps to the scaffold, and Sir Amyas Paulet offered his arm to the Queen to assist her in the ascent. "I thank you, sir," she said, with graceful courtesy, as she accepted his help: "it is the last trouble that I shall give you, and the most acceptable service you have ever rendered me."

She stepped upon the scaffold and sat upon the chair provided for her. The two Earls walked on either side of her; and, in front of her, was the executioner, clad in black velvet, and holding his axe with the edge turned towards her. His assistant stood beside him. She saw them, and the block, and the crowd in the hall, thirsting for her blood; and she saw it all without betraying any trepidation or fear. The eye-witnesses of the scene testify that she "regarded the

* I was able to give Miss Agnes Strickland a copy of the music believed to have been played on this occasion. It was discovered, in manuscript, at Oxford, and is the old tune called "Jumping Joan," which, in those days, was played to brutalise the rabble at the burning of a witch. It is remarkable, however, that when the tune is played in slow time, it produces a solemn and pathetic effect, and is very similar to the "Dead March" in *Saul*. Miss Strickland thinks that the tune may have been played to slow time, at Fotheringhay (Vol. viii, p. 487). A charitable supposition, but scarcely in accordance with the indignities and insults that characterised the tragedy. (For further notes on this subject, see Miss Strickland's letter to me, in the Appendix to this book.)

assembly with a joyous countenance;" and that when Beale stepped on the platform and read her sentence of death, "she listened unto it with as small regard, as if it had not concerned her at all, and with as cheerful a countenance as if it had been a pardon from her Majesty for her life." And yet, the biassed historian Froude brutally calls this a piece of "brilliant acting"—"a dramatic sensation"—by "a bad woman, disguised in the livery of a martyr." The "livery of a martyr" is something new in word-coinage! There is not a tittle of evidence to shew that she could have hoped for either reprieve or rescue. The military guard surrounding the scaffold rendered a rescue impossible; while a reprieve was hopeless.

Beale ended the reading of the death-warrant, and the Queen of Scots bowed her head in token of submission to the will of God. Then said the Earl of Shrewsbury, "Now, madam, you know what is to be done." "Do your duty!" she replied. Then she addressed the assembly, that, although she was a sovereign princess, and not subject to the Parliament of England, she had been unjustly accused of crimes of which she was altogether innocent. She had never devised any harm against the Queen of England; and she believed that, after her execution, much would be brought to light that was now hid, and that the objects of those who so eagerly sought her death would be disclosed. From her heart she pardoned all her enemies, and her tongue should not utter that which should turn to their prejudice.

She then asked for her almoner, that she might pray with him: but, her request was refused; and Dr. Fletcher, Dean of Peterborough, came to the rail and delivered a lengthy, tiresome, and ill-timed harangue, which, as reported by Lord Burghley's commissioner, occupies four pages in Archdeacon Bonney's "Fotheringhay." Suffice it to say here, that it stated, that the Queen's most excellent majesty, notwithstanding all her trespasses against her sacred person, state, and government, had yet a tender care for her soul, and was anxious for her salvation, and that she should be brought into the true fold of Christ, out of the communion of that church in which if she remained, she must perish everlastingly.

She stopped him—or endeavoured to stop him—more than once, by requesting him not to trouble himself in the matter, as she was resolved to die in her own faith.

Then she turned from him; but he would not be put off; and went round the scaffold, and again facing her, continued his harangue. At last, the Earls were constrained to put an end to this extraordinary scene: and commanded him to cease his exhortation and to begin to pray.

The Dean, kneeling upon the steps of the scaffold, offered up the following prayer:—

"O most gracious God, and merciful Father, who, according to the multitude of thy mercies, dost so put away the sins of them that truly repent, that thou rememberest them no more; open, we beseech thee, thine eyes of mercy, and behold this Person appointed unto death, whose eyes of understanding and spiritual light, albeit, thou hast hitherto shut up, that the glorious beams of thy favour in Jesus Christ do not shine unto her, but is possessed with blindness and ignorance of heavenly things (a certain token of thy heavy displeasure, if thy unspeakable mercy do not triumph against thy judgment), yet O Lord our God, impute not, we beseech thee, unto her those her offences which separate her from thy mercy; and if it may stand with thine everlasting purpose, and good pleasure, O Lord, grant unto us, we beseech thee, this mercy which is about thy throne, that the eyes of her heart may be enlightened, that she may understand, and be converted unto thee; and grant her, also, if it be thy blessed will, the heavenly comfort of thy Holy Spirit, that she may taste and see how gracious the Lord is. Thou hast no pleasure, good Lord, in the death of a sinner, and no man shall praise thy name in the pit; renew in her, Lord, we most humbly beseech thy majesty, whatsoever is corrupt in her, either by her own frailty, or by the malice of the ghostly enemy: visit her, O Lord, if it be thy good pleasure, with thy saving health, as thou didst the offender at the side of thy Cross, with this consolation: 'This day shalt thou be with me in Paradise:' Say unto her soul, as thou didst unto thy servant David, I am thy salvation; so shall thy mercy, being more mighty, be more magnified. Grant these mercies, O Lord, to us thy servants to the increase of thy kingdom and glory, at this time. And further, O most merciful Father, preserve, we most humbly beseech thy majesty, in long and honourable peace and safety, Elizabeth thy servant, our most natural Sovereign Lady and Queen; let them be ashamed and confounded, O Lord, that seek after her soul; let them be turned backward, and put to confusion that wish her evil. And strengthen still, Lord, we pray thee, the hand and balance of justice amongst us, by her gracious government; so shall we, both now and ever, rest under thy faithfulness and truth, as under a shield and buckler, and bless thy name and magnify thy mercy which liveth and reigneth one most gracious God for ever. Amen."

Mary heard but little or nothing of this prayer. She sat upon the low stool provided for her, and engaged in devotion, praying aloud ("with powerful, deep-chested tones?" says Froude), in Latin, from Psalms 31, 51, and 91, having her crucifix in her hands, and, at her girdle, a pair of beads, with a gold cross at the end. Her women were weeping and wailing around her, and, sliding from her stool, she knelt on the cushion, and prayed again, not only in Latin, but also in French, and then in English. She prayed for herself—for Christ's afflicted Church—for her son—for Queen Elizabeth, and for peace and prosperity to England and Scotland. Then, rising from her knees, and holding up her crucifix, she said "As Thy arms, O Christ, were extended on the cross, even so receive me into the arms of Thy mercy, and blot out all my sins with Thy most precious blood."

With inconceivable insult, the Earl of Kent told her, that "it would be better for her to eschew her popish trumperies, and bear Christ in her heart."

She meekly replied, "Can I hold the representation of my crucified Redeemer in my hand, without bearing him, at the same time, in my heart?"

The two executioners then, according to custom, knelt down to ask forgiveness of what they had to do. "I forgive you," she said, "with all my heart; for, I hope this death will give an end to all my troubles."

The executioners then, with an eye to perquisites, began to attempt to disrobe her; but, she stayed their advances, saying, with a smile, that she had never had such grooms to wait upon her before, nor had she ever disrobed before so numerous a company.

She then beckoned to her maids, Jane Kennedy and Elizabeth Curle, who were kneeling outside the scaffold. They went to her, but were so overcome by their emotion that they could render her but little help, and she herself took out the pins from her dress. As they continued weeping, she placed her finger to her lips, to command their silence, saying to them, "Do not weep! I am very happy to leave this world. You ought to rejoice to see me die in so good a cause."

They then assisted her to disrobe, taking off her chain of gold pomander beads, and laying her crucifix on the stool. The chief executioner seized it as his perquisite; and Jane Kennedy, after a struggle, snatched it from him.

"Friend!" said Mary to him, "let her have it; she

will give you more than its value in money." It was the rosary she had bequeathed to the Countess of Arundel, and it is still possessed by Mr. Howard, of Corby Castle.

She then took a final farewell of her weeping ladies, who were crossing themselves and praying. She also, as they knelt at her knees, signed them with the cross, and bidding them farewell, prayed them to pray for her to the very last.

Divested of her outer garments, she now appeared in the petticoat and laced camisole of crimson velvet, and covered her arms with a pair of crimson velvet sleeves. Thus, she appeared attired from head to foot in crimson.* Then she knelt, while Jane Kennedy bound round her eyes a gold-bordered handkerchief and *Corpus Christi* cloth in which had been the consecrated wafer. Having pinned this, the two maidens were compelled to descend from the scaffold, leaving their royal mistress alone to close up the tragedy of her life.

"Then the Queen," wrote the eye-witness to Burghley, "kneeled down upon the cushion, at which time, very resolutely, and without any token of the fear of death, she

* Or as Froude says, "blood-red from head to foot." Carrying out his theory of a theatrical performance, he adds, "Her reasons for adopting so extraordinary a costume must be left to conjecture. It is only certain that it must have been carefully studied, and that the pictorial effect must have been appalling." He says, "she stood on the black scaffold, with the black figures all around her." Except her own maidens, there is no evidence that there were any black figures besides the two executioners in black velvet. But Mr. Froude is nothing, unless picturesque.

EXECUTION OF MARY, QUEEN OF SCOTS.
(From an old print.)

spake aloud this Psalm (XXXI.) in Latin, "In Te, Domine, speravi, ne confundar is œternum," &c. Then, groping for the block,* she laid down her head, putting her chain over her back with both her hands, which, holding there still, had been cut off, had they not been espied. Then she laid herself upon the block most quietly, and stretching out her arms and legs, cried out "In manus tuas, Domine," &c. ("Into Thy hands, O Lord, I commend my spirit!") three or four times. At last, while one of the executioners held her straightly with one of his hands, the other gave two great strokes with the axe, before he did cut off her head, and yet left a little gristle behind; at which time she made very small noise, and stirred not any part of herself from the place where she lay."

Dr. Lingard, Miss Strickland, and Mr. Hosack, quoting from other authorities, say that the executioner struck three times; and that, at the first stroke, he inflicted a deep wound on the lower part of the skull. Any way, two strokes or three, the butchery was done in a terribly bungling manner.

"Then," continues the eye-witness in his account to

* Tennyson ("Queen Mary,") describing the execution of Lady Jane Grey, says:

"And when her innocent eyes were bound,
She, with her poor blind hands feeling—'where is it?
Where is it?'"

Burghley, "the executioner which cut off her head, lifted it up, and bade 'God save the Queen;' then her dressing of lawn fell from her head, which appeared as grey as if she had been three score and ten years old, poled very short, her face being, in a moment, so much altered from the form, which she had when she was alive, as few could remember her by her dead face: her lips stirred up and down almost a quarter of an hour after her head was cut off."

"Then, said Mr. Dean, "So perish all the Queen's enemies." And, afterwards, the Earl of Kent came to the dead body, and standing over it, with a loud voice likewise said, "such end happen to all the Queen's and the Gospel's enemies."

"Then one of the executioners, pulling off part of her dress, espied her little dog, which was under her clothes, which could not be gotten forth but by force, and afterwards would not depart from her dead corpse, but came and laid between her head and shoulders (a thing diligently noted:) the dog being imbrued with her blood, was carried away and washed, as all things else were that had any blood, except those things that were burned. The executioners were sent away with money for their fees, not having anything that belonged to her. Afterwards, everyone was commanded forth of the hall, saving the sheriff and his men, who carried her up into a great chamber, made ready for the surgeons to embalm her,—and there she was embalmed."

So ends the account of the tragedy by the eye-witness who signed himself "R. W.," and despatched by him, three days after the execution, to "The Right Honourable Sir William Cecil, Knt., Lord Burleigh, Lord High Treasurer of England."

"See the last morning break! with mournful state,
Forth comes the royal captive to her fate.
Death could not move her grief—the sighing breath
Of pitying bosoms gave the sting to death.
'Be calm!' she said, 'for Stuart soon shall be
Above the sphere of mortal majesty;'
Her little triumphs and her wrongs be o'er:—
Weep, no more, Melvin—faithful,—weep no more!
A trembling hope her last sad words express;
Scotland admonish, ruthless England bless,
But, oh! the pause that follow'd—and the groan
Struck ev'ry nerve, and froze the blood to stone!" *

"Thus" says Sir Walter Scott, "died Mary, Queen of Scots, aged a little above forty-four years. She was eminent for beauty, for talents and accomplishments, nor is there reason to doubt her natural goodness of heart, and courageous manliness of disposition. Yet, she was, in every sense, one of the most unhappy Princesses that ever lived, from the moment when she came into the world, in an hour of defeat

* "Antona's Banks": (1797.)

and danger, to that in which a bloody and violent death closed a weary captivity of eighteen years. * * This may be truly said, that, if a life of exile and misery, endured with almost saintly patience, from the 15th of June, 1567, until the day of her death upon the 8th of February, 1586, could atone for crimes and errors of the class imputed to her, no such penalty was ever more fully discharged than by Mary Stuart."

Dr. Robertson, the historian, says "Mary's sufferings exceed, both in degree and in duration, those tragical distresses which fancy has feigned to excite sorrow and commiseration: and, while we survey them, we are apt altogether to forget her frailties; we think of her faults with less indignation, and approve of our tears as if they were shed for a person who had attained much nearer to pure virtue."

Brantome wrote of her; "No man ever beheld her person without admiration and love, or will read her history without sorrow."

Even the biassed Froude is compelled to say of her last moments, "The self-possession was faultless, the courage splendid. Never did any human creature meet death more bravely."

Renauld de Beaulne, Archbishop of Bourges, and Patriarch of Acquitaine, in his funeral oration at the special service held in Mary's memory, in the Cathedral of Nôtre Dame, Paris, in March, 1587, spoke, most eloquently, of her endowments, whereof "it was not easy to find so many centred in one human being; for, besides that marvellous beauty which attracted the eyes of all the world, she had a disposition so excellent, an understanding so clear, and judgment so sound, as could be rarely paralleled by a person of her sex and age. She possessed great courage, but it was tempered by feminine gentleness and sweetness." He described the splendours of her bridal day in that Cathedral at the early age of fifteen,* and then said: "A little time has flowed on, and it has all vanished like a cloud. Who could have believed that such a change could have befallen her who appeared then so triumphant, and that we should have seen her a prisoner who had restored prisoners to liberty; in poverty, who was accustomed to give so liberally to others; treated with contumely by those on whom she had conferred

---

* Thus referred to by Tennyson, in his *Queen Mary*, where the Queen says to Noailles,

"Mary of Scotland—for I have not own'd
My sister, and I will not—after me
Is heir of England; and my royal father,
To make the crown of England one with ours,
Had mark'd her for my brother Edward's bride;
Ay, but your king stole her a babe from Scotland
In order to betroth her to your Dauphin.
See then:
Mary of Scotland, married to your Dauphin,
Would make our England, France."

honours; and, finally, the axe of a base executioner mangling the form of her who was doubly a Queen; that form which honoured the nuptial bed of a sovereign of France, falling dishonoured on a scaffold, and that beauty which had been one of the wonders of the world, faded in a dreary prison, and at last effaced by a piteous death."

Miss Agnes Strickland says, "With the notorious exceptions of Queen Elizabeth, Catherine de Medicis and the Countess of Shrewsbury, Mary had no female enemies. No female witnesses from her household came forward to bear testimony against her, when it was out of her power to purchase secresy if they had been cognisant of her guilt. None of the ladies of her court, whether of the reformed religion or of the old faith—not even Lady Bothwell herself—lifted up her voice to impute blame to her. Mary was attended by noble Scotch gentlewomen in the days of her royal splendour; they clave to her in adversity, through good report and evil report; they shared her prisons, they waited upon her on the scaffold, and forsook not her mangled remains till they had seen them consigned to a long-denied tomb."

Mr. Robert Chambers, in his "History of Scotland," says of the prisoner of Fotheringhay: "Her extraordinary misfortunes, confinement, and its attendant bad health, together with the influence of her religion, had reduced her mind to a degree of soberness and gravity very different from what it displayed in the days when life was young and hope in its prime. She now regarded death rather as a blessing than an evil, for it promised her a passage from a labyrinth of miseries, which she could never otherwise hope to leave behind her. Thus, while Elizabeth cherished towards her those malignant feelings which a wolf may be supposed to entertain towards the prey he is about to rend asunder, Mary prayed with sincerity and fervour for the happiness of her destroyer; and even, after having given up all hope of life, was able to write to her in a strain of almost sisterly affection."

Such was the end of the tragedy of Fotheringhay.

The following poem on the Execution of Mary, Queen of Scots, was written by my friend, the Rev. George Edmond Maunsell, Rector of Thorpe Malsor, near Kettering: *

"She heard unmoved the fatal message told,
Her cheek blanched not, nor ran the life-blood cold
Back to the sickening heart; but as a queen
She bore her, whilst around her maids were seen
In all the frantic attitudes of woe.

* He died, Oct. 29, 1875, aged 60, at Marina, St. Leonard's-on-Sea. A volume of his "Poems" was published, in 1861, by Smith, Elder, and Co.

One, bending downwards, rocks her to and fro;
One stands as all aghast: no breath, no moan,
Betrays another's grief, but marble, stone,
She sits, while from the eyes like thunder rain
The tears plash down; one, starting up amain,
Shrieks, bans and curses. Near, the Kentish chief
Turns down his wolfish eyes, as when a thief
Gripped in the act stands sullen, or some sprite
Of hated darkness, by the enchanter's might
Forced up to outer day, with evil glance
Glares from his downcast eyelids all askance.

"'Tis sudden," were the words Queen Mary spoke,
"Sudden, but not less welcome comes the stroke
That ends my sorrows; yet I scarcely deemed
That she, my sister—she who surely seemed
Throned to love mercy, justice and defend
The suppliant and the stranger—thus should bend
Her thoughts to slay the stranger, the opprest.
Yet be it so—to me the change is blest,
Nor deem I worthy of eternal bliss,
The shrinking soul that, at such time as this,
Bears not the body up through that short strife
That bars the passage to eternal life.
But mine stands fix'd and firm—although, perchance,
In girlhood's days, in happy, blithesome France,
Some natural dread had been, some tears had passed
To hear to-morrow's sun must be my last.
Now, all is o'er, mine own familiar friends
Against me draw the sword; a dark cloud bends
O'er Scotland's royal race; and all I pray,
Is that from Mary's blood some happier day
May dawn on Stuart's name. For England's Queen
I have unfeign'd forgiveness: none, I ween,
Deem gentlier of her deed. 'Tis sure no wrong

To grant the freedom I have sighed for long.
Weep not! to-morrow all shall see that I,
As Christian and as Queen know how to die;
Nor deem them for myself, if trace of tears
On this wan cheek at early dawn appears;
My spirit joyous stirs, and in this breast
Pants but to flee away and be at rest."

The fatal hour is come, that morning's red,
Whose eve shall see thee numbered with the dead,
Wronged Mary Stuart! All death's hideous gear—
The axe, the block, the headsman—wait thee near.
Yet still, with heart unstirred, with look serene,
Moves onward to her death fair Scotland's queen.
Calm she unrobes her, calmly bends and prays
For England's queen—success, and length of days
For her who shortens hers. "Tell each true heart"
(These her last words) "that firmly I depart
Fixed in the ancient faith: I know no wrong
That I have done to any; but ere long
Before His throne, we, face to face, shall plead,
Who sees the secret thought clear as the deed.
There I repose my trust: His doom shall tell
Mine innocence or guilt—and now, farewell!"

'Tis done! one bigot voice is heard alone,
"Thus die Eliza's foes!" One sullen tone
Singly replies "Amen!" The heaving breast,
The starting tear-drop, show how feel the rest.

O Mary Stuart! gentlest of thy race,
Unmatched in form and loveliness of face!
How can we deem thee guilty, yet survey
Thy last calm hours, when hope had passed away!
Surely, no sullen apathy of crime
Bore up thy spirit in that awful time;

Not the dull consciousness of hidden guilt,
But, thy firm trust on Jesu's mercy built,
Bade thee, with Faith's strong eye, the future scan,
And hope that mercy here denied by man.
In the dark shadow of that gloomy vale,
Where e'en the mightiest spirits bend and quail,
There wast thou proved, there counted to be pure;
Thence hast thou passed in innocence secure,
Safe from the smiter's hand, the oppressor's rod,
Wafted on seraph wings to meet thy God.

PART IV.

FUNERAL OF MARY, QUEEN OF SCOTS.

THE bloody work was done, and the butchery was over. Elizabeth's victim was dead, though the lips in the severed head still moved, and the body was warm and palpitating. Jane Kennedy and Elizabeth Curle, regardless of the pools of blood, sprang on the scaffold, and besought the executioners "not to strip the corpse of their beloved mistress, but to permit her faithful servants to fulfil her last request, by covering it, as modesty required, and removing it to her bedchamber, where themselves and her other ladies would perform the last duties."

Needless to say, their prayer was not granted. They were rudely repulsed, hustled out of the banquet-hall, and placed under lock and key. The executioners, to secure their perquisites, began to rudely strip the body, but were not permitted to take anything that had belonged to the murdered Queen. They had to satisfy themselves with a money fee. The portions of the dress over which her blood had gushed, were thrust into the fire, together with the black cloth from the block and stool, so that none might dip handkerchiefs in the royal blood, or preserve any fragments for relics. The decapitated body was coarsely wrapped in the cloth that had been stripped from the billiard-table, and was carried out of the hall to an upper chamber. The hall was cleared of its spectators; and Lord Talbot, son of the Earl of Shrewsbury, rode off at a gallop to take to the Queen, at Greenwich, the joyful news that her victim was dead. The London bells rang out merrily, and bonfires blazed, as soon as the tidings were made known that the prisoner of Fotheringhay was now a corpse.

Meanwhile, the decapitated head of Mary was carried, on the black velvet cushion, to the large window of the banquet-hall, where, for the space of an hour, it was exposed to the view of the throng of visitors and soldiers in the courtyard. One of the spectators, most probably, was Amyas Cawood (brother or nephew of Margaret Cawood) who painted the picture of the severed head of Mary Stuart, which came into possession of Sir Walter Scott, and is in the collection at Abbotsford. It is depicted as placed on a table, covered with scarlet cloth, and bears the artist's name, with the inscription: "Maria Scotiæ Regina, February 9th, 1587." Miss Strickland describes the picture thus:—"This affecting posthumous portrait bears an unmistakable analogy in features and contour to Mary's prison pictures; but the nostrils are sharpened and a little elevated. A solemn stillness appears to have composed the marbled brow, placid lips and sealed eyelids, and the grey pallor of death supersedes the beautiful tints of her natural complexion. One pearl appears among the dark locks which have been replaced by the artist, and the brow is adorned with a radiated diadem—the martyr's crown. The delineation of the neck is considered anatomically true, and is a terrifically fine work of art; yet, it is impossible to contemplate the ineffable composure of the features,

> 'And mark the mild angelic air
> The rapture of repose that's there,'

without feeling that it verifies its own authenticity, by bringing Mary Stuart's countenance before us at the blessed season 'when the wicked had ceased from troubling, and the weary was at rest.'"

Another portrait, probably from another eye-witness, of the severed head of Mary Stuart, is in the Museum of the United Service Club. A full length portrait of the Queen of Scots, presumably the work of Amyas Cawood, is in the Scotch College at Paris, whither it came from the Scotch College at Douay, to which college it had been presented by Elizabeth Curle. A steel engraving of this portrait is given in Miss Strickland's last volume of "Mary Stuart"; and a copy of the painting is in the Royal collection at Windsor. It represents the Queen of Scots as she appeared upon the scaffold; and, in the background, is a vignette representation of the scene of the execution, after the first blundering stroke of the axe had made a ghastly wound on the base of Mary's skull. The likenesses and costumes of those on the scaffold are believed to be very exact. Thus, both in painting and writing, there is much contemporaneous evidence of the tragedy in the banquet-hall at Fotheringhay.

With reference to Mary's hair, close cut and grey, the Earl of Shrewsbury said that it had been so cut in his house for the convenience of applying cataclasms to relieve her severe headaches. These were neuralgic, and were, probably, the chief cause of her hair turning prematurely grey. Lord Byron, however, thought otherwise, for, in his note to "Manfred," where he complains that he is

"Grey-haired with anguish,"

he mentions, as instances, Marie Antoinette, and Mary, Queen of Scots, turning rapidly grey "with cares and sorrows"; and that the hair of Mary's grandson, Charles I, turned quite grey, in like manner, during his stay at Carisbrooke. In another place, Byron says,

"But, there are forms which Time to touch forbears,
And turns aside his scythe to vulgar things,
Such as was Mary's, Queen of Scots: true—tears

And love destroy: and sapping sorrow wrings
Charms from the charmer, yet some never grow
Ugly."

Mr. Froude—always eager to detract—says, "At once a metamorphosis was witnessed, strange as was ever wrought by wand of fabled enchanter. The coif fell off and the false plaits. The laboured illusion vanished. The lady who had knelt before the block was in the maturity of grace and loveliness. The executioner, when he raised the head, as usual, to show it to the crowd, exposed the withered features of a grizzled, wrinkled old woman." It is self-evident, that the "maturity of grace and loveliness" could not instantly be transformed into the extreme opposite, even by the cruel work of the axe. That her face was "in a moment, so much altered from the form which she had when she was alive," was only natural, and we can well believe the eye-witness of the scene, when he made this report to Burghley. But, for the sake of strong contrasts, Mr. Froude deviates from the stern facts of the case—which, in any form, are sufficiently odious and repugnant.

Sorrow, sickness, treachery and weary years of captivity had, as a matter of course, left their traces on the face and form of Mary, Queen of Scots, of whom the historian, Dr. William Robertson, says: "With regard to the Queen's person, a circumstance not to be omitted in writing the history of a female reign, all contemporary authors agree in ascribing to Mary the utmost beauty of countenance and elegance of shape of which the human form is capable. Her hair was black, though according to the fashion of that age she frequently wore borrowed locks, and of different colours. Her eyes were a dark grey,* her complexion was exquisitely fine, and her hands and arms remarkably delicate, both as to shape and colour. Her stature was of a height that rose to the majestic. She danced, she walked, and rode with equal grace. Her taste for music was just, and she both sung and played upon the lute with uncommon skill."

With regard to the affecting episode of Mary Stuart's little pet dog accompanying her on the scaffold, hidden by her train, and refusing to leave the severed head of his mistress, Miss Strickland says that the dog was a Skye terrier, and that "some barbarous fanatic, desiring to force a verification of Knox's favourite comparison between this unfortunate Princess and Jezebel, tried to tempt the dog to lap the blood of his royal mistress; but, with intelligence beyond that of

---

* "And when you add to this, her womanhood
In its meridian, her blue eyes or grey—
The last, if they have soul, are quite as good,
Or better, as the best examples say;
Napoleon's, Mary's (Queen of Scotland) should
Lend to that colour a transcendent ray;
And Pallas also sanctions the same hue,
Too wise to look through optics black or blue."

Lord Byron.

his species, the sagacious creature refused; nor, could he be induced ever again to partake of food, but pined himself to death." This she gives on the authority of Teulet's "La Morte de la Royne d'Escosse." The dog is shewn, underneath Mary's dress, in the engraving of "Queen Mary on the scaffold blessing her ladies," from the picture by Gourlay Steell, A.R.S.A., in the seventh volume of Miss Strickland's "Lives of the Queens of Scotland." The incident was also used to advantage by Sir Edward Bulwer Lytton:—

"And not one human eye:—yet see, what stirs the funeral pall?
What sound—a sound of sorrow—wails low moaning through the hall?
Close by the world-forsaken form, one thing a vigil keeps,
At every sound without, more near to that still'd heart it creeps:
It gazes on those glazed eyes—it hearkens for a breath—
It does not know, poor fool, why Love should not be true to Death.
It still can fawn, as fond a slave, upon that powerless hand;
It still can hear from voiceless lips, a voice that can command.
To that alone, through all the earth, no matter what had been,
The pomp or fate, the guilt or doom—the Dead was still a Queen."

After the headless body of the murdered Queen, wrapped in the cloth from the billiard-table, had been carried from the scaffold in the banquet-hall, to an upper chamber in Fotheringhay Castle, it was there embalmed, either on the same, or the next, day, by a physician from Stamford, assisted by the Fotheringhay apothecary, in the presence of Paulet and the Sheriff. As Mary's almoner had been denied admittance to the scaffold, so her surgeons were denied admittance to her corpse. Nor were her faithful maidens allowed to see the body of their mistress; for, as soon as it had been embalmed, it was placed in a leaden coffin.

For six months, that leaden coffin remained in that upper chamber at Fotheringhay; and, for six months, the servants of the murdered Queen were kept close prisoners; during which time, as Sir Walter Scott says, "Queen Elizabeth, in the same spirit of hypocrisy which had characterised all her proceedings toward Mary, no sooner knew that the deed was done, than she hastened to deny her own share in it. She pretended that Davison had acted positively against her command in laying the warrant before the Privy Council; and that she might seem the more serious in her charge, she caused him to be fined a large sum of money,* and deprived him of his offices, and of her favour for ever. She sent a special messenger to King James to apologize for "this unhappy accident," as she chose to term the execution of Queen Mary."

She asserted, that "she was neither consenting to, nor

* £10,000: see Charles Knight's "Old England," p. 55. See also Lingard's "History," where there is a singular misprint, at p. 474,—not corrected in the table of *Errata*—that Davison was released "from confinement in 1689." It should be 1589.

cognisant of, the barbarous deed that had been perpetrated on her unfortunate kinswoman at Fotheringhay." In short, it was an "unhappy accident." When the Earl of Sinclair, appeared, clad "in complete steel," before Mary's son, James enquired if he had not seen the order for a general mourning. "Yes," was the high-spirited reply: "this is the proper mourning for the Queen of Scotland."

For six months the headless body of the Queen of Scots, lay, in its leaden casket, in that chamber in Fotheringhay Castle: when, at last, yielding to the remonstrances of Mary's son, and the appeals of her faithful servants, Elizabeth granted permission for the body of her victim to receive Christian burial. More than this, she ordered that the obsequies should be conducted with state ceremonials, and that Peterborough Cathedral should be the scene of the funeral. The first of August, 1587, was the day fixed upon for the ceremony.

Some days before that date, Mr. Fortescue, Master of the Grand Wardrobe, Garter King-of-Arms, was sent down, with Mr. Dorrel, and Mr. Cox, and other officials, to make the needful arrangements both at Peterborough and Fotheringhay. Other officials, with a milliner, were also sent to Fotheringhay, with black cloth and requisite material for mourning-cloaks and head dresses, for Sir Andrew Melville,

Burgoigne, and the ladies who had attended on the Queen of Scots not only at Fotheringhay, but also at Chartley, from whence they had been brought to Fotheringhay and there detained during the past six months. These preparations, however, were unavailing, for all the attendants of the late Queen declared that they would only wear the mourning that they already had in use.

On the evening of Sunday, July 30th, the Garter King-of-Arms, with five heralds, and forty horsemen, arrived at the Castle, bringing with them a funeral car, drawn by four caparisoned horses. The car was covered with black velvet, on which were escutcheons bearing the arms of Scotland, with little pennons round about it. The leaden coffin, placed in an outer coffin, was carried down the stairs, and lifted on to the car, by torch-light, by the bareheaded heralds, habited in their coats and tabards. Then, at ten o'clock, the procession started for Peterborough, by torch-light, and a mourning train of men and women, who had been faithful to the Queen of Scots in the days of captivity, followed her murdered remains as they were borne away, in mock state, from Fotheringhay Castle, her last prison, and the scene of her sham trial and cruel death.

It must have been a weird scene, in the dead of the night, to any one who chanced to see that torch-light procession making its slow way along the country roads. The villages of Elton, Chesterton, Alwalton, Orton Waterville, Orton Longueville (a seat of the premier Scottish Marquis—the Marquis of Huntly), and Woodstone, would have to be passed, before the bridge over the Nene to Peterborough was reached. The distance was about ten miles, or rather more; and it was between one and two o'clock, in the early morning of Monday, July 31st, that the procession halted before the west door of Peterborough Cathedral. The body was there received by the Bishop, (Richard Howland) the Dean and Chapter, and Clarencieux, King-of-Arms, and was borne to the vault, not without difficulty, for it weighed nearly nine hundred weight, and the embalming had been done in such a defective way, that it was feared the leaden coffin might burst.

The place selected for the vault was in the south aisle, near to the tomb of John, the last Abbot and first Bishop of Peterborough, and immediately opposite to that of the ill-treated Queen, Katharine of Arragon, the first wife of Mary's uncle, King Henry VIII. Queen Katharine's hearse of black and silver was still standing over her grave, which had been dug by Robert Scarlett,* the Sexton, who also dug the

* He died July 2, 1591, aged 98, having buried two Queens, and two generations of the inhabitants. A very interesting portrait—exhibited at

grave for Mary Stuart. Except for any silent prayers from the real mourners, Mary's faithful attendants, the coffin was placed in the vault without any ceremony—the state ceremonial being reserved for the following day. The vault was immediately covered, a small opening only being left to receive the broken staves at the time of burial. The cost for breaking the ground and making the grave was ten pounds, and twenty pounds was spent on black hangings of baize, ornamented with metal escutcheons, that were hung in the Choir, and on every second pillar of the Nave.

---

the Portrait Gallery, South Kensington, in 1866—hangs on the west wall of the nave of Peterborough Cathedral, and its removal to some more appropriate building is much to be desired. Underneath the portrait are the following lines:—

"You see old Scarlett's picture stand on hie,
But, at your feet here doth his body lye.
His gravestone doth his age and death-time shew,
His office by heis token you may know.
Second to none for strength and sturdy lymm,
A scare-babe mighty voice, with visage grim;
He had intered two queenes within this place
And this townes householders in his life's space
Twice over, but at length his own time came,
What he for others did, for him the same
Was done: no doubt his soule doth live for aye,
In heaven, though here his body clad in clay."

He is represented as wearing a red skull-cap, brownish red jacket and trunk hose, blue stockings, and red-heeled black shoes tied with blue ribands. His spade is in his right hand; a bundle of five keys in his left; and his dog-whip stuck through his girdle. The present painting was reproduced from the original in 1747. (See Murray's *Eastern Cathedrals*, p. 71; Rev. O. W. Davys' *Guide to Peterborough Cathedral*, p. 72; Rev. W. D. Sweeting's *Parish Churches in and around Peterborough*, p. 62; Rev. G. A. Poole's *Diocesan History of Peterborough*, p. 148; Chambers' *Book of Days*, Vol. II, p. 17.)

On the Monday afternoon, the ceremonial state mourners reached Peterborough from London, and were sumptuously entertained in the Bishop's Palace. The Countess of Bedford was the representative of Queen Elizabeth, as chief mourner; which, of course (says Miss Strickland) "must be regarded as a public acknowledgment that Mary was innocent of all the crimes laid to her charge, especially that of practising against the life of Elizabeth."

A great supper was given to these state mourners in the Bishop's banqueting-hall, which was hung with black—the Countess of Bedford being seated on a throne of state, beneath a purple velvet canopy. Sir Andrew Melville and Burgoigne were brought into the hall to see these preparations, and were told that "her Majesty wished no expense to be spared," and "if they thought that there was anything that required altering or amending." To which they coldly replied, "It is not for us to find fault, the whole being dependent on the pleasure of the Queen, your mistress, who is, doubtless, discreet enough to make proper preparations."

Early on the morning of Tuesday, August the first, the Bishop's Palace was astir. Soon after eight o'clock, the Countess of Bedford, attended by the lords and ladies, was escorted, by the Bishops of Peterborough and Lincoln, from her own chamber to the presence-chamber, where, under a cloth of estate, the staves of office were given to the Lord Chamberlain and the other officers. Then, with her train borne by Lady St. John, and, with the Earls of Rutland and Lincoln on either side, Elizabeth's representative walked in procession to the Bishop's banquet-hall, there to find, according to custom, a representation of the murdered Queen lying upon a bier.

The sham body was then borne by six cloaked gentlemen, with eight gentlemen carrying bannerols, and four knights bearing a canopy, and was carried from the Palace to the Cathedral. The order of the procession is given at length in Gunton's "History of Peterborough Minster," but is too long to be quoted here. Suffice it to say, that many hundreds of officials, titled persons, gentlewomen, poor men, and poor women were there; and that the helm and crest, and target and coat-of-arms, and other heraldic emblems, were borne in the procession, as at a royal funeral.

It was received, at the Cathedral, by the two bishops, the dean and the clergy, and carried to the southern entrance to the choir. There, over the vault, wherein the real body was laid, the sham body was placed under a gorgeously decorated hearse, twenty feet square by twenty-seven feet high, with escutcheons and fringe of gold. Over the sham coffin, a pall of black velvet was thrown, and a gold and jewelled crown was placed on a purple velvet cushion. Among the mourners were "seventeen Scots in cloaks; and a Scottish priest," who is said to have been De Préan, Mary Stuart's almoner. He had a gold cross pendent at his breast. Burgoigne, and all the Scots, except Sir Andrew Melville and the two Mowbrays, then withdrew from the Cathedral, not wishing to join in a service to which they were aliens; and this conduct offended many of the English present, who endeavoured, vainly, to force them to remain.

Then, the Bishop of Lincoln, Dr. William Wickham, preached a sermon from the fifth and three following verses of the 39th Psalm, "Lord, let me know mine end," &c. When, in his prayer, he gave thanks for those who were translated out of this vale of misery, he used these words, "Let us give thanks for the happy dissolution of the high and mighty Princess, Mary, late Queen of Scotland, and dowager of France, of whose life and death, at this time, I have not much to say, because I was not acquainted with the one, neither was I present at the other. I will not enter into judgment further; but, because it hath been signified unto me that she trusted to be saved by the blood of Christ, we must hope well for her salvation; for, as Father Luther was wont to say, 'many a one that liveth a Papist, dieth a Protestant.'" Which extraordinary prayer, he then followed up by an ordinary discourse on the general doctrine of the vanity of all flesh. But, even this prudent discourse was adjudged by the fanatical Puritans to contain expressions that were too favourable to "the popish Princess;" and Martin Marprelate* charged the Bishop of Lincoln with praying that his soul, and the souls of all the rest there present, might be with the soul of that unrepentant papist departed.

At the close of the sermon, a long piece of velvet and a cushion were laid at the Bishop's feet, for the Countess of Bedford to kneel upon. She was conducted to it by the King of the Heralds and four officers with white staves, the Earls of Rutland and Lincoln being on either side of her, and her train being borne by Lady St. John. She knelt awhile before the Bishop, and then returned to her former seat. The coat armour was then brought from the hearse, and taken by the two Earls to the Bishop, and then laid on the altar. The sword, helmet, target, crown and crest were treated in the same manner; and two red banners were also

* This was the assumed name of John Ap Henry, a Welsh fanatic, and a furious denouncer of the Crown and Church. His scurrilous pamphlets were provided by himself at his own press, which he set up at various places. At the date of the Queen of Scots' funeral, he was living at Fawsley, in Northamptonshire, where he worked his printing-press in a private upper room, approached by a winding-stair. He was brought before the Star Chamber Court and heavily fined; but, this did not deter him from speaking seditiously against Queen Elizabeth, for which crime he was executed, May 29, 1593. (See Maskell's *History of the Mar-Prelate Controversy.*)

laid on the altar, and the eight bannerets were placed in the hearse. The Countess, her train borne by Sir John Manners, then advanced a second time to the Bishop, "and offered;" followed by the ladies and gentlemen two-and-two, and the officers with white staves. The Bishop of Lincoln was then conducted from the pulpit; and the greater part of the mourners then left the Cathedral. Towards the door of the choir, the Scottish women stood, parted on either side; and, as the English ladies passed, they kissed them all.

Then the Dean read the funeral service at the vault, the officers breaking their staves and casting them upon the coffin. This ended the ceremony; and the procession returned to the Bishop's Palace, where a handsome banquet was prepared to which the attendants of the murdered Queen were invited. They refused to go, saying that "their hearts were too sad to feast, and they preferred being by themselves, as they could not restrain their tears from falling." Their wish was granted; and they dined by themselves in a separate room, no Englishmen being present but those who served them, and who noticed that "they took no pleasure in their banquet, and wept more abundantly every time they were pressed to eat."

In the afternoon the nobility quitted Peterborough, where the concourse of people was so great as to amount to several thousands. Thus ended the state ceremonial of the removal of Mary's corpse from Fotheringhay to Peterborough. For six months it had not found a grave at the castle prison; and its occupancy of the cathedral vault was only temporary. As the Queen of Scots' body, in life, had been taken from one prison to another, so was it with her body after death. Five-and-twenty years passed away; and the murdered form then received another royal funeral. It was exhumed from the vault in Peterborough Cathedral, and removed by her son, King James, to Westminster Abbey, there to finally rest, in the centre of the south aisle of Henry VII's chapel.

The stately monument erected by her son to her memory, shews her reposing beneath a regal canopy, her head resting on cushions, and the Scottish lion at her feet. The face is considered to be a genuine likeness, corresponding in feature, contour, and expression, with the best authenticated portraits. The face is lovely and intellectual; the form, graceful and majestic. "As long" says her French biographer, Caussin, "as there shall be eyes and tears in this vale of misery, there shall be tears distilled on those royal ashes, and the piety of the living shall never cease, with full hands, to strew lilies, violets and roses on her tomb."

The following touching poem on the funeral of Mary Queen of Scots, in Peterborough Cathedral, was written by my old friend, John Plummer,* and may fitly close this narrative.

"Aye, crown her *now*, poor murder'd Queen;
  Ye titled mourners kneel,
And simulate the grief and pain
  Your hearts could never feel
When, in her prison wretchedness,
  For liberty she sighed,
Or strove in vain, with tears and prayers,
  To melt the Tudor's pride.

Let tapers blaze and pennons wave,
  And wardens line the hall;
Let shields display their antique charms
  Above the sombre pall:
What boot they now, these honours rare,
  This royal pomp and state?
Can they restore the dead to life,
  Or close the scroll of fate?

* Who, having successfully floated over a whole "sea of troubles," and surmounted difficulties that would have appalled a less resolute and industrious nature, after a hard, but noble, literary career in England, is now reaping the fruits of his well-earned harvest of fortune, in a distinguished position in Australia. In the beautiful home that he has made for himself in the neighbourhood of Sydney, and which he has named after a place (Thorpe Malsor) very dear to him in the old country, he has had the satisfaction of seeing his sons following in their father's footsteps; and with the happy surroundings of wife and family, he finds himself deservedly honoured and respected. When resident at Kettering, Mr. Plummer wrote much concerning Fotheringhay and other places of note in the neighbourhood. The poem of "The Funeral of Mary, Queen of Scots," was published in his *Songs of Labour, Northamptonshire Rambles, and other Poems*, issued from the local press at Kettering, in 1860, in a volume gratefully dedicated to Lord Brougham, and containing an autobiographical sketch of the author's life, and his early struggles as a factory operative. John Plummer was my companion in a visit to some of the places described in this book, and he told me, that when he was in Scotland, he saw, offered for sale, many snuff-boxes that were described as being made of wood brought from Fotheringhay.

Can they recall the early days,
  So joyous and so blest,
When France's gay and sunny soil,
  Her feet in gladness prest?
Through all the splendour and the glare
  Which mark the gorgeous scene,
Who can forget the headsman's axe—
  The pale and murder'd Queen?

And *thou*, stern Queen, whose jealous hate
  Thus ruthlessly could doom
The lovely rival of thy crown
  So early to the tomb;
If ever sigh from broken heart
  May dare against thee plead,
Beware! lest thou, in life's last days,
  Seek mercy in thy need.

For, more of Love, and more of Truth,
  Thy helpless victim knew,
Than ever thou in all thy pride,
  Around thy throne might view.
'Tis not the rank nor yet the gold
  That can affection move,
A gentle mind and kindly heart
  Alone we learn to love."

PART V.—CONCLUDING REMARKS.

THE faithful attendants of Mary, Queen of Scots, were rigorously treated, even after this mockery of a state funeral. For six months, during the whole of the time that the unburied coffin of their murdered mistress was kept in the upper room in Fotheringhay Castle, they had been detained there as prisoners. And now that their attendance at the funeral was over, they were escorted back from Peterborough to Fotheringhay, and again made prisoners, being denied air and exercise, and barely supplied with the necessaries of life. This confinement extended for nearly three months, when Mary's son sent Sir John Mowbray, Baron of Barnbougal, and father of Barbara and Gillies, to the court of Elizabeth to demand their release. The request was granted: and the French attendants went to France, and the Scotch to Scotland, with the exception of Gillies Mowbray, Mrs. Curle and Elizabeth Curle, who joined Sir John Mowbray, in London. Afterwards, Mrs. Curle, with her husband and Elizabeth, went to Antwerp, where they spent the rest of their days, Elizabeth presenting to the Scotch College of Douay, that full-length portrait of Mary Stuart on the scaffold, of which I have already spoken. Jane Kennedy married Sir Andrew Melville, and was drowned in crossing in an open boat from Barntisland to Leith, when she was proceeding to meet King James's bride, Anne of Denmark, and bring her to Scotland, in the year 1589.

Shortly after the funeral of Mary, Queen of Scots, an epitaph, written by Mr. Blackwood, in Latin, was placed over her grave. Here is the translation of it:—"Mary, Queen of Scots, a King's daughter, widow of the King of the French, cousin and next heir to the Queen of England, adorned with royal virtues and a royal mind—the royal authority being often implored in vain—by the barbarous cruelty and tyrannical sentence of the English, the ornament of our age and the true royal light, is extinguished. And, by the same nefarious judgment, both Mary, Queen of Scots, hath suffered a natural death, and all other Princes (made plebeian) suffer a civil death. A new and unheard of kind of tomb is this, in which the living are included with the dead. Know, with the sacred ashes of the divine Mary, here lies prostrate and violate the majesty of all Kings and Princes. And, because this silent, royal monument abundantly admonishes Kings of their duty, traveller, I say no more."

Such very plain out-spoken words could not be permitted to remain, and the tablet was soon removed; but, by whose orders, is not known. When Dugdale visited the grave, in

1641, he made a drawing of the Helmet and Escutcheon, which were still pendant over the vault; but, they were destroyed during the great rebellion.

Referring to the murder at Fotheringhay,* Camden, as a contemporary writer, was compelled to use discretion: and he guardedly says, "As for that disastre which even heere (Fotheringhay) befell unto another most mighty Prince *Mary* Queene of Scots, I had leifer it should be enwrapped up in silence, than once spoken of: Let it be forgotten quite, if it be possible: if not, yet be it hidden, as it may in silence. Under the best Princes some there are who being once armed with authority, know how by secret slights to set a goodly shew and fair pretense of conscience and Religion, thereby to cloke their owne private designes: And there be againe, that sincerely and from the heart tender true Religion, their Princes security, yea and (which is the highest rule and law of all) the publique safety. Neither can it bee denied,

* In a curious little book, "Metrical History of England for Young Persons," (Ballantyne and Hughes, Edinburgh, 1844,) wherein it is presumed that the chief facts in English History can be best taught "young persons" in very doggerel rhymes, we are treated to the following lines concerning Queen Elizabeth, and her real reason for putting Mary Stuart to death:—

"Fear of Rome led
Her to behead
In Fotheringhay Tower,
The beauteous Queen
Of Scots who had been
Years prisoner in her power."

but that even the best Princes themselves are otherwiles violently carried away, as good Pilotes with tempests, against their wils whither they would not. But what they doe as Princes and Kings, let us leave to God who onely hath power over Kings."

So wrote the discreet historian, unwilling to speak the truth concerning his Queen. "No scandal against Queen Elizabeth, we hope!" seems to have governed his mind and his pen. He wrote "Pilotes," though he might have written Pilates. But, that murderous tragedy in the banquet-hall at Fotheringhay could never be "forgotten quite, if it be possible." It is one of those deeds burnt into the brain, and impossible to be forgotten, however much we might desire for the scene to be closed in oblivion.

Mr. John Hosack, Barrister-at-law, in his vindication of Mary, Queen of Scots, says,* "The history of Mary Stewart has left so indelible a stain upon that both of England and Scotland, that we need not be surprised to find a majority of the writers of both countries agreed as representing her as the victim of her own misconduct. Although it is natural to sympathise with misfortune, national pride and religious prejudice are sentiments far stronger; and nothing could be more

* "Mary, Queen of Scots and her accusers." Second Edition, Blackwood; 1874. Vol. II, 488-496.

humiliating to both than the reflection that an innocent woman had undergone a course of persecution to which all similar examples of State iniquity are but as dust in the balance. But, there are three English historians of the seventeenth, eighteenth and nineteenth centuries respectively, who have arrived at this conclusion, and who, in point of research and accuracy, are certainly unequalled by any of their contemporaries." These are Camden, Carte, and Lingard. The conclusion at which these historians have arrived is strongly corroborated by a very important authority, the late Mr. Markham J. Thorpe, who was employed of recent years by the Master of the Rolls to peruse and arrange the vast collection of letters and papers relating to the Queen of Scots, contained in the Record Office. After examining and arranging all these documents, he expressed himself as follows: "the evidence they contain is all-important; there is abundance of insinuation, there is much assertion of guilt, *but proof nowhere*, so far as the compiler has been able to seek it. * * * *

"Those historians who maintain that the Scottish Queen was the victim, like so many of her ancestors, of her turbulent and treacherous nobility, have a comparatively easy task to perform: but those who have adopted what may be called the popular view of the question, have an obvious difficulty in presenting to their readers an intelligible notion of her character and conduct. The caricatures of Knox and Buchanan have at least the merit of consistency. They deny her the possession of a single virtue, and they accuse her of every crime. But these extravagant creations have given place to others still more extravagant. The favorite fashion at present seems to be to paint her at once as the worst of criminals and the most estimable of her sex. Kindly yet cruel—constant in her attachments, yet treacherous and fickle,—generous and confiding, yet perfidious alike in planning and remorseless in executing her deeds of vengeance,—Mary Stewart has been presented to modern readers as a paragon of contradiction, resembling nothing else in history or even in fiction.

"In this estimate of the character of the Scottish queen, Hume, the ablest and most indulgent, and Mr. Froude, the most recent and most reckless of her modern adversaries, seem to agree. "The most amiable of women" is an expression that slips, as it were, involuntarily from the pen of Hume when summing up the qualities of Mary. Mr. Froude, although he denounces her as the worst and most abandoned of her sex, and in language unprecedented among historians of any age, nevertheless informs his readers that she was "warm and true in her friendships," that she had "a noble nature," and that she was "generous" in the extreme. It is difficult to see what more could be said even by the most devoted of her admirers. * * * * *

"Yet in the darkest hours of her existence, even when she hailed the prospect of a scaffold as a blessed release from her protracted sufferings, she never once expressed a doubt as to the verdict that would be finally pronounced between her and her enemies. "The theatre of the world," she reminded her judges at Fotheringhay, "is wider than the realm of England." She appealed from her persecutors to the whole human race, and she has not appealed in vain. In regions uninhabited and unknown when she uttered these words—on the ice-bound shores of the Baltic, in the busy cities of the Far West—the story of her life creates as deep an interest as in the capitals of Europe; and, so long as beauty and intellect, a kindly spirit in prosperity and matchless heroism in misfortune, attract the sympathies of men, this illustrious victim of sectarian violence and barbarous statecraft will ever occupy the most prominent place in the annals of her sex."

Carte, the French historian, says of the royal prisoner at Fotheringhay, "The patience, the constancy, the firmness with which she endured all the hardships and indignities put upon her during her captivity, cannot be sufficiently admired; the Christian manner of her death was not unworthy of the best of men; and the intrepidity with which she met the King of terrors, the genuine effect of innocence, was not surpassed by any of the heroes of antiquity."

A life and vindication of Mary Stuart was written by Samuel Roberts, the philanthropist, and friend of James Montgomery, the poet. When Sheffield Lodge or Manor House—in which Mary had been imprisoned, was destroyed, Mr. Roberts secured the stones of her bedroom window, and placed them in a tower, erected to her memory, in his own grounds at Park Grange. His daughter, Miss Mary Roberts, wrote a volume of poems "The Royal Exile," descriptive of the Queen of Scots' imprisonment at Sheffield; and Mr. Roberts, then in his eightieth year, penned the following lines on Queen Mary's window:—

"Alone, here oft may Scotia's beauteous Queen,
Through tears, have gazed upon the lovely scene,
Victim of villainy, of woman's hate,
Of fiery zeal, of wiles and storms of state;
Torn from her throne, her country, and her child,
And cast an exiled monarch on this wild,
She here was taught, what youthful beauty ne'er,
While seated on a throne, had deign'd to hear,
To say, submissive, at the closing scene,
'Tis well, that I have thus afflicted been!'
Then, calmly, on the block, in faith, resign
Three heart-corrupting crowns, for one divine.
Reader!—the ways of God are not like thine!"

It was from such a prison window, that the banker-poet,

Samuel Rogers, imagined the Queen of Scots to have gazed, in his "Pleasures of Memory."

"So Scotia's Queen, as slowly dawned the day,
Rose on her couch, and gazed her soul away.
Her eyes had bless'd the beacon's glimmering height,
That faintly tipped the feathery surge with light;
But now the morn with orient hues portrayed
Each castled cliff and brown monastic shade:
All touched the Talisman's resistless spring,
And, lo, what busy tribes were instant on the wing!
Thus kindred objects, kindred thoughts inspire,
As summer-clouds flash forth electric fire."

"Sir," said Dr. Johnson to Boswell, in the Advocates Library at Edinburgh, "never talk of your independency, who could let your Queen remain twenty years in captivity, and then be put to death, *without even a pretence of justice*, without your ever attempting to rescue her. And, such a Queen, too! as every man of any gallantry of spirit would have sacrificed his life for!"

Even Wesley, in his Journal (April, 1768) defends the Queen of Scots and asserts her innocence. "But how then," he continues, "can we account for the quite contrary story which has been almost universally received? Most easily. It was penned in French, English and Latin (by Queen Elizabeth's order) by George Buchanan, who was secretary to Murray, and in Queen Elizabeth's pay; so, he was sure to throw dirt enough. Nor was she at liberty to answer for herself. But, what then was Queen Elizabeth? As just and merciful as Nero, and as good Christian as Mahomet." This is, probably, as severe a sentence on the English Queen as was ever penned; and, coming from such a man, the condemnation is all the more sweeping.

Sir Walter Scott said, "While Elizabeth fluctuated, not between remorse and desire of committing the crime, but concerning the mode in which it should be accomplished, Mary prepared herself for death with all the dignity of a Queen, and the firmness of a martyr."

The Rev. G. R. Gleig said, "Never was a piece of acting more clumsily performed, because no one was deceived by it. Elizabeth intended from the first that Mary should die; and her sole regret was, that there should not be found among her loving subjects, persons willing to sacrifice both honour and life, in order that her character might be screened from the ignominy of participating in the execution."

"It is but too clear," says Mr. Charles Knight, "that Elizabeth wished the unhappy prisoner made away with secretly, in order, no doubt, that she might deny all participation in her death afterwards. * * * In spite of the continual failure of her endeavours before the execution, to ensure a scapegoat who should bear the odium of Mary's death, Elizabeth was not the less determined to have a victim afterwards, who might at least seem to have been the most guilty party. Of course, the very man who had kept her from the perpetration of the murder she had really wished, was the very man to suffer now for the execution that she had to profess she had not wished—not intended to have taken place. So, poor Davison, instead of being let off, like Burghley and the others, with a show of royal displeasure, was utterly ruined by a fine of ten thousand pounds, and his committal to the Tower for the whole of the remainder of the reign."

I conclude this *catena* of criticism with the following general remarks from the accomplished and sympathetic pen of Miss Agnes Strickland.

"The name of Mary Stuart has thrown that of every other Queen of Scotland into the shade. She appears to represent in her single person the female royalty of that land, having absorbed the interest pertaining to all the other princesses who, previously to her brief reign, presided over the courts of Dunfermline, Stirling and Holyrood. Mary Stuart is, exclusively, the Queen of Scots—Queen, not only of the realm, but of the people; and, with all her faults, real or imputed, she remains to this day the peculiar object of national enthusiasm in Scotland. Her memory haunts the desolate palaces where every peasant is eager to recount traditionary lore connected with her personal history. Not a castellated mansion of the sixteenth century but boasts of some quaint-looking room, which is emphatically pointed out as Queen Mary's chamber. Every old family possesses a painting, for which the distinction of an original portrait of Queen Mary is claimed. Tresses of every shade of golden, auburn and chestnut, are preserved and fondly exhibited as "well-attested portions of her hair." Persons who denounce the relic veneration of the Romish Church as idolatrous, enshrine a glove, a fan, a superannuated watch, or any other trinket supposed to have belonged to Queen Mary, among their choicest treasures, to be handed down as heir-looms in their families. The variety of articles thus preserved and hallowed for her sake, is almost incredible. Queen Mary's mirrors and cabinets appear interminable; and as to the antique chairs of carved oak and ebony with which their present possessors have endowed her, they are numerous enough to supply seats for all her descendants, who, be it remembered, are to be found on almost every throne in Europe. More books have been written about Mary Stuart than all the queens in the world put together; but * * * it is only now in the fulness of time, that a succinct narrative of personal facts and characteristic traits could be arranged, containing particulars of every period of her life, from the hour of her birth to the dark closing of the tragedy in the hall of Fotheringhay Castle."

Dr. Lingard, quoting from the narrative of "the young, fair Mrs. Southwell, sworn Maid of honour to Queen Elizabeth," states that for several days before her death, on March 24, 1603, Elizabeth lay on the floor of her chamber for many days and nights, positively refusing, though entreated by her attendants to return to her bed. If they had seen, she told them, what she had seen there, they would not have asked her to go back to bed. Cecil told her that she must do so, to satisfy her people. "Must!" she cried; "is *must* a word to be addressed to princes?" To the Lord Admiral she said "I am tied with an iron collar about my neck." And so, for some days, till she breathed her last, still lying on the cushions on the floor. Who can doubt, but that among the visions that haunted her bed, was the murdered form of the royal prisoner of Fotheringhay?

Appendix.

ORIGINAL LETTERS
OF
MISS AGNES STRICKLAND.

In connection with the subject of "Fotheringhay, and Mary, Queen of Scots," I will add some extracts from letters written to me by Miss Agnes Strickland, from her family residence, Reyden Hall, near Wangford, Suffolk,—chiefly in the year 1853,—when she was writing her life of Mary, Queen of Scots, which occupies five volumes of her "Queens of Scotland," published, at intervals, by William Blackwood and Sons, 1852-6. I especially value my copy of the work, as being "the gift of the authoress," for whom I made various water-colour drawings of Fotheringhay, Oundle and Conington. She thus acknowledges their safe reception:—

"I hasten to acknowledge the safe receipt of your beautiful and curious antiquarian drawings, which came to hand unscathed by post-bag pressures and collisions with hard or heavy substances; a special piece of good fortune; for, I have had so many nice drawings spoiled in that way. I must now thank you very heartily for them; and, above all, for the good will to Queen Mary and her biographer, which inspired you with the generous impulse of devoting so much of your time and charming talent for sketching historical antiquities, to our service. I am very glad that you have not been at the trouble of mounting them; as I keep a book, "in velvet bound, and broidered o'er," for the reception of everything I can catch illustrative of my royal mistress, Mary Stuart; and these drawings of yours will be most valuable additions, and are more acceptable unmounted, because mounted drawings are apt to strain the binding.

"I should be very sorry to put the broad R— or Arrow mark of Crown appropriation—on your interesting communication touching the Fotheringhay chair of State, especially as it will be a year or more ere I come to that dismal climax of my history. So, pray use your own pleasure on the subject of *Notes and Queries*.

"Conington Castle is a very picturesque drawing, and I am enchanted with that of the old Inn at Oundle, which reminds me of the New Inn at Gloucester, built in Edward III's reign, for the accommodation of the pilgrims who came to pay their devotions at his murdered father's tomb in the fair Cathedral."

Three weeks after this, Miss Agnes Strickland wrote to me the following very interesting letter:—

"Before I sit down to my diurnal labour, in preparing the portion of Mary Stuart's life and reign, which, at present, engages my whole thoughts, and almost makes me forget Agnes Strickland, I have entered into a covenant with myself to perform your requisition; and having extricated your last very interesting letter from its temporary fastenings in my Mary Stuart correspondence book, I am happy to be able to comply with your wish by return of post.

I know, too well, the impossibility of replacing from memory lost papers of graphic descriptions, where a mistake would be almost fatal to the reputation for correctness, which every antiquary and historian is anxious to preserve. I feel too much indebted to you for the beautiful drawings, and the trouble you have taken in illustrating them with your minute descriptions, to think of the abstraction of a few minutes from my own business to oblige you, and only hope you will kindly return the manuscript to me when you have quite finished with it.

Many thanks for the funeral march,* which, I think, must be the same I heard in Scotland; but, as I have given up

* See page 122.

practice, for want of time, and got rid of our old rattle-trap piano, in order to make room for bookcases and cabinets, I shall not be able to ascertain that point to a certainty, till I call upon a musical friend a few miles off, and get her to play it over two or three times to me. My impression is that this march must have been composed for her grand funeral in Peterborough Cathedral, in which case, its performance would have been duly authorised. But, in none of the records of her execution, have I ever seen mentioned that there was any kind of music. Still, I am far from discrediting the tradition. I think some little search into the old music scores of Peterborough Cathedral, might tend to throw light on the composition of this beautiful and affecting air.

I shall feel greatly obliged by your courtesy in making the transcript from Gunter's "History of Peterborough;" and, perhaps, if not asking too great a favour, you would kindly write on one side of the paper only.

In respect to portraits of Mary Stuart, there is a curious one in the old Episcopal Palace at Gloucester,* with an inscription of later date asserting that it is a likeness of Queen Elizabeth, whom it resembles in nothing but the costume,

* There was one in the Episcopal Palace at Ely, where, in 1850, the Bishop (Dr. Turton) shewed it to me, and told me that he always took it with him in the carriage when he went up to London, and brought it back again with him. C. Bede.

and superabundance of jewels. If you ever go to Gloucester, and mention my name to Mrs. Hughes, sister-in-law to the Bishop of Gloucester, also a friend of mine, I am sure she would allow you to see it; and, if you possess the same charming talent for copying portraits as you do for original delineations of architectural antiquities, you might find it well worthy of your pencil. I should have had a reduced copy in water-colours made for my book, if there had been an artist at hand capable of producing a faithful delineation of the really beautiful features. I suspect that the wrong name was purposely added in the days of Charles I, to preserve the picture from being cut, or otherwise injured, by the puritan destructives of that barbarous period, who hated and persecuted the memory of Mary Stuart. I believe I was the first to detect the fraud—if so it may be termed—which assigned to Elizabeth features and contour of face, which she could not have purchased at the cost of her royal diadem—the darkly delicate complexion, chestnut hair, and eyes of almond form, the dark expressive and lengthened curve of Mary Stuart's majestic eyebrows, long aquiline nose, and pouting lips, round chin, and perfectly oval face.

The painting, though sadly out of repair, is really good, and has a depth of shade which Mary's correct artistical taste approved, and Elizabeth forbade, by an order of Privy

Council, ever to be used in the attempts made by any artist to delineate her august countenance; although it would have been a loyal service to have toned down her light red hair, and faintly curved eyebrows; to have given some depth to her round, telescopic, pale, blue eyes; and to have relieved the baldness of her forehead and pear-shaped visage; to say nothing of the improvement that it would have been to her thin retreating lips, to have added a few marking touches to the chin.

However, I must conclude in haste, having scribbled more than prudence warrants at present, from, dear Sir,

Reyden Hall,
Wangford,
Suffolk.
February 2, 1853.

Your sincerely obliged
AGNES STRICKLAND.

In October of the same year, (1853,) she wrote to me asking my acceptance of "the newly published volume of my life of Mary Stuart," and again mentioned the Gloucester portrait.

"I have succeeded in obtaining a sketch for engraving from the fine old portrait of her at Gloucester Palace, wrongly lettered Elizabeth, and I mean to use it as the frontispiece for the next volume.

"During a tour, made by me last summer, I visited Tutbury Castle, a very extensive ruin, and observed a plant of the royal thistle of Scotland growing on the sloping bank of the moat, much degenerated in height and size from the parent plants in Scotland. At Derby, my attention was attracted by a noble Elizabethan mansion in Babington lane, called Babington Hall, where the royal prisoner slept one night; but I had not time to gratify my desire of examining the interior of the mansion. I understand the Inn where she slept at Coventry is still in existence, and hope to visit both the last-named places next year.*

"You will rejoice to hear that I have discovered papers in the State Paper Office, which must fully establish her innocence of the foul charges with which her enemies have maligned her. Any fresh illustrations of antiquities from your able pencil, illustrative of her English localities, will be acceptable to, dear Sir, Yours very sincerely

AGNES STRICKLAND.

* She, subsequently, found that "this ancient hostelry—the Black Bull Inn, in Smithford Street, near the gateway of the Greyfriars, just within the entrance of the town—was demolished at the close of the last century, and the present barracks were erected on the site. The officers' rooms occupy the site of the apartments where Queen Mary and her ladies were confined from the 25th of November till December 9th, 1569. Coventry was, at that period, surrounded by massive walls, fortified with thirty towers and gates." But, the Castle was in a ruinous state, not having been repaired or inhabited since the Wars of the Roses; therefore, Lords Shrewsbury and Huntingdon, after vainly endeavouring to obtain more suitable quarters, were compelled to house themselves and their prisoners at the Black Bull Inn. Queen Elizabeth wrote angrily to the two Earls, "that they had carried the Scottish Queen to an Inn, which is very inconvenient even for the name's sake." She, and her attendants, were accordingly removed from the Inn to the mansion called the Mayoress's Parlour, adjoining St. Mary's Hall; and their apartments are still preserved.

Writing to me, in the following month, November 8th, from Edinburgh, she says,

"You ask me "what I think of you" in regard to the postponement of the promised sketch of Fotheringhay. To which I reply, "that I suppose your time has been more profitably employed; and that I shall be very happy to express my grateful sense of your unmerited liberality, in devoting any specimen of your charming talent to my service and that of Mary Stuart." Come when it may, and in whatever shape, it will be acceptable. "The smallest contributions gratefully received."

"I am leaving Edinburgh to-morrow for Lennox Lene, near Haddington, on a short visit to my charming friends the Dowager Lady Blantyre, and her daughter, Miss Stuart. Like Pilgrim, I shall carry my burden at my back, in the shape of the proofs of the last three chapters of Mary Stuart's life—or rather, for I have not got her to Fotheringhay Castle yet, of her reign. This Vol. V, Queens of Scotland, ends with her abduction; and she will come out as bright as truth can make her. I feel that truth is anything but acceptable to vulgar minds, and that a very vigorous concert of braying will be sent forth from the Exeter Hall-ites: but, in that case, I hope my reviewers will get well *Punch*-ed by those who wield the pencil and the pen with equal skill." *

* She was aware that I was then contributing to *Punch* both with pen and pencil.

She added a "P.S. A lady's mind! please when you send the promised drawing, direct it to the old address, Reyden Hall, Wangford, Suffolk."

I failed to send the sketch at the appointed time; and, writing to me, in the ensuing Christmas, she said,

"Pray use your own time and convenience in regard to the drawings and local information with which you so kindly promise to favour me, I have another volume of Mary Stuart to complete before I enter the fatal ground of Fotheringhay; so, there is not the slightest cause for haste; and, even if it were otherwise, I should be sorry, indeed, for any earthly consideration to interfere with your duties to your congregation, at this season, when the benificence of her ministers and members, is wont to serve the cause of our own Apostolic Church better than ten thousand per-cent of railing at the errors of other religious communities can ever do. *Amor vincit omnes.*"

In another letter, she refers again to *Punch*, and says, "I shall not petition you to give a sly *punch* to my assailants, unless they are more vituperant than becomes fair foes; but, just to keep the No-Popery-howlers in order, when they falsely, and injuriously, raise a cry of "papist," for want of anything else to say against me and my royal heroine. As for poor Mary, I believe it was the villainy of Moray, and the ill manners of Knox, that kept her from being the Queen of a reformation established on better grounds than that of spoliation of churches and church-lands. As for me, her humble biographer, I have ever been a sincere member of the Church of England—a church that enjoins true witness, by exhorting us from her altar not to bear false,—an article of the decalogue little regarded by Mary's foes or mine.

"I shall be charmed to receive any sketch, or sketches, from your able pencil, illustrative of Fotheringhay. I have a pretty drawing of the keys and the arch from Archdeacon Bonney's illustrated copy of his history of Fotheringhay.

"I wish you would perpetrate a few historical caricatures in the way of Kirkpatrick Sharpe's Queen Elizabeth dancing to the sound of a small fiddle in her seventieth year. I think the righteous Regent Moray, and the other covetous professors of holiness, making their selections from Mary Stuart's rich wardrobe and jewel-house for selves and wives, would be a nice subject. The pearls, the richest in the world, were packed up and sent to Queen Elizabeth for her to purchase at one third of their value. These should be in a tray by themselves, with a ticket "For the Queen of England." Moray's Countess, a little mean-looking vixen, whose picture is decorated with one of Mary's regal frontlets, should be putting it on and coaxing her husband for it. Knox looking on, in horror at their vanities.

"Two of the Maries were threatened and bullied by Morton and Lennox, to give up "certain rich gowns, jewels and furs," which they had in their keeping; and were, finally, forced to surrender them to those robbers. There might be one scene especially representing their restoration. But, wait till you get my next volume, and turn the idea in your mind."

In acknowledgment of a royal thistle, and some fragments of stone from the foundations of the banquet-hall of Fotheringhay, Miss Agnes Strickland wrote to me,

"Many thanks for your friendly exertions to put me in possession of a genuine root of the Scotch royal thistle from the ruins of Fotheringhay Castle; but I must be contented with a few of the seeds, since the plant is only a biennial, and will not bear transplanting. Perhaps when you have an opportunity of sending to London, you would kindly address your parcel of relics to me at Avenue Lodge, Portchester Gardens, where my sister has a nice cottage and garden; and, for the present, we could add the Fotheringhay stones to her little rock there, and her maid would take charge of them for me."

In another letter, she returns to the subject of the royal thistle, and says,

"I am charmed with the legend of the thistle of Fotheringhay, and always find a great charm in local traditions, which, if not always true, are at least the shadows of truth. No shadow can appear without a substance causing it. Mary was a horticulturist and a poet. I should imagine she sowed the seeds of the royal thistle of Scotland in the gardens of her English prisons. I should like to ascertain whether they are to be found at Tutbury."

Subsequently, she informed me that they were to be found there: and that, if Mary herself did not sow the seeds, her admirers may have done so.

"I have the pleasure of sending you the first volume of my life of Mary, which you have richly deserved; and I shall be happy to send you the other volumes, as a small acknowledgment for your beautiful drawings. You will see my opinion about the colour of Mary's hair in my description of the frontispiece. It is dark in the Gloucester portrait, misnamed "Elizabeth." I imagine that portrait, from the costume, must have been one of the few painted while she was Darnley's wife. You will observe that her widow portraits are all in black and white, with a lawn cap. This at Gloucester is in regal costume."

In another letter she thanks me for my sketch and description of the chair preserved in Conington Church, and says,

"I know your chivalry in the cause of the beautiful and illustrious victim. I should like you to make a pictorial sketch of the reading of the death-warrant on the scaffold, which she sat calmly to hear, with the headsman, the axe, and the block before her, the two Earls standing by, and her weeping maids, Jane Kennedy and Elizabeth Curle, behind her.* What a subject it would make! I have some thought of having it for the vignette of my last volume.

"The Dean and Chapter of Peterborough have King James I's autograph letter for the removal of her body to Westminster Abbey. I should be glad of a transcript of it for my book.

"I am working very hard, and hope to get it to press in March; but, the labour is intense, and begins to tell on my health and spirits."

I obtained the copy of the letter of James I, and sent it to Miss Strickland. She wrote,

"Many thanks for your friendly services in obtaining for

* They do not appear to have been on the scaffold till a little later, when they endeavoured to assist their royal mistress in her last preparations. C. B.

me the copy of the letter for the removal of Queen Mary's remains from Peterborough Cathedral. I now want to trace the particulars of the removal, the names of the persons employed, and the manner and order of the procession to London, and reception in Westminster Abbey: and the ceremonial of her body being consigned to the vault in the royal south aisle Chapel of the Abbey; and the date. These particulars would be most interesting, because entirely unknown to historians of the present day; but I cannot find any clue to them."

I was able to help her to some of these points; and she wrote,

"I am very much obliged to you for your great kindness in taking so much trouble in working out the points I want to ascertain. I suppose, from your pretty little map, the royal remains would proceed through Stilton and Hatfield, towards London, by the old North Road. * * *

"On the subject of the removal of Queen Mary's body. I feel very much indebted to you for taking so much trouble for me. I continue very much occupied on this volume; but hope, by the end of this month (February) to send the larger portion of the MSS. to press; but, the particulars touching the removal of the body, will not come in this; only I like to be prepared for them. With repeated acknowledgments for all your friendly acts of attention. Believe me to be, dear Mr. B—,

Yours sincerely,

Agnes Strickland.

A few days after this, (February 21, 1856,) she wrote to me as follows,—

"I can do no less than acknowledge the safe arrival of your exquisite sketches of Fotheringhay, by return of post, and, after thanking you, most sincerely, for so precious an addition to my material for the last chapter of my biography of Mary Stuart, express my admiration of these beautiful and spirited sketches, which I have placed, with equal pride and pleasure, in my royal Stuart Album, among other mementoes of the murdered Mary which I am collecting.

"Your descriptions of those local features are very interesting and graphically done, convincing me more and more that your talents ought to be devoted to a higher branch of literature than comedy. Your style is so clear and pleasant, and rises with the subject. I am charmed with the interest excited on the subject of the chair at Conington. I think you might get up, with these beautiful sketches and a few others, a charming little volume on Fotheringhay and its recollections and local features, which would sell well along that line and to travellers to Peterborough. I once travelled that route before the line was opened, in a carriage from Bloxholme, in Lincolnshire, where I had been spending a few weeks with Lady Mary Christopher, and remember the Church, the mound of the Castle, and the windings of the river Nene, being particularly interested for Mary's sake; but, as it was a cold November day, we did not quit the carriage, till we arrived at Peterborough, where I made my first pilgrimage to Mary's grave.

"I have seen the old thin history of Fotheringhay, which, however, contains nothing important.*

"I have often tried to get the particulars of Mary's re-interment at Westminster; but, though the fact is always mentioned, I have never been so fortunate as to obtain any of the details, in the numerous histories of Westminster Abbey I have consulted. However, there is nothing like returning to the charge, which I shall do before I send my last chapter to the press.†

"Mrs. Monk, the wife of the Bishop of Gloucester, told me, "the blind King of Hanover, when he visited the Abbey, expressed the greatest desire to visit Mary's tomb, and made particular enquiries, passing his hand over everything she described to him, and tracing the profile with his finger,

* Archdeacon Bonney would not have been pleased with this criticism on his work! C. B.

† She was unable to obtain the particulars.

which, he said, "must have been very beautiful." After having lingered there some little time, with an air of the deepest interest. he said, as he turned away, "I think I shall remember all about Mary Stuart's tomb!" wishing, at the same time, that he could have seen it.

"This, I think, argued sensibility and good feeling on his part."

This anecdote is particularly interesting. In reply to something that I told Miss Strickland, relative to Mary's escape from Lochleven, as narrated to me by a descendant of the Douglas, she replied,

"George Douglas was, probably, about Queen Mary's age. His father, Sir Robert Douglas, was killed at the battle of Pinkie, 1547, when Mary was in her fifth year: so that he must, in 1567, have been turned of twenty, and might have been much older. Willie Douglas was the boy of sixteen who effected her deliverance. Sir Walter Scott, in his romance of "The Abbot," confounds these characters; but, they were very distinct personages. George was a strong protestant.

"I am progressing with the forthcoming volume of "Mary Stuart," and hope it may be out in May: but, it is desperate hard work."

In another letter on various matters, she says of her work,

"When I am occupied with Mary Stuart, I have little leisure for anything besides." In another, she again refers to Archdeacon Bonney's work; "Thanks for the extracts touching Fotheringhay. Archdeacon Bonney lent me his illustrated and interleaved copy: but, I was disappointed, expecting more than I found. I had a delicious tour in Scotland, and returned to finish the old year, and begin the new, with my dear mother. I am now, as you suspect, deeply occupied with the conclusion of my life of Mary Stuart. Half the volume is in type; but I have still four chapters to arrange."

In another letter, she mentioned her discovery of deeds, shewing that the word "Perio" was in use earlier than Mary Stuart's time: but, I have already referred to that point, in my history of Fotheringhay, and I was able to state it, on Miss Strickland's authority, in my papers, published in *The Leisure Hour*, November, 1865. I sent a copy of the magazine to Miss Strickland, who, dating from "Park Lane Cottage, Southwold, Suffolk, November 18, 1865," thus acknowledged it: "I have much pleasure in reading your very interesting papers on Fotheringhay, in "The Leisure Hour," which I shall cut out, and lay by among my collections for a new edition of that volume of Mary. Not that I shall be able to use more than a few sentences of your valuable local information."

I think that this is all that I need quote from Miss Agnes Strickland's very interesting letters to me, on the subject of this volume. She was an excellent and vivacious correspondent; and her letters to me were on a great variety of themes; private and family matters; her own works, "The Queens of England," "The Bachelor Kings of England," her historical novel, "How will it end?" &c.; the clique of critics who always "wrote her down," and against whom she inveighs in somewhat strong terms; my own literary productions, "Verdant Green," &c., with my West Highland books, "Glencreggan," "West Highland Stories," and "Tour in Tartanland," in which Mary Stuart was several times mentioned: the value of copyrights—dealings with publishers, with her own personal experiences thereupon. Her eldest sister, Elizabeth, also wrote to me on this subject. She is unknown to fame, but greatly assisted her sister in the researches required in the history of "The Queens of England"—the work by which Miss Agnes Strickland will, probably, be best known; although the five volumes of her "Life" of Mary Stuart, with two supplementary volumes of "Letters," must be regarded as her second best historical work, and a remarkable and able vindication of the character of the beauteous and fascinating Queen of Scots.

Sir Archibald Alison's high panegyric on Miss Agnes

Strickland, is, that she is "a lady who stands at the head of her whole sex, in all ages, in historical literature." Another critic said of her, "Intellectually, she is one of the three exceptional women of the Victorian age. If Mary Somerville was the Urania, and if Elizabeth Barrett Browning was the Erato, Agnes Strickland is certainly the Clio of our generation." The Essayist in *Blackwood's Magazine* summed up her merits as a historian, thus—"Miss Strickland's talents as a writer, and turn of mind as an individual, in a peculiar manner fit her for painting a historical gallery of the most illustrious or dignified female characters in that land of chivalry and song (Scotland). In her delineations of individual character, Miss Strickland evidently takes the greatest pains to be impartial; and the multitude of new documents and facts which she has brought on both sides of the question, in regard to her heroines, is a sufficient proof that this most laudable principle is a ruling one in her mind."

Her "Lives of the Queens of Scotland" were in eight volumes, the publication of which extended over a period of ten years (1850—9), and the Life of Mary, Queen of Scots, occupied five of these eight volumes. In it, she brought forward many new facts, having had access to hitherto-unpublished documents in the Register House, Edinburgh, the State Paper Offices of London and Paris, the collections of the Earl of Moray, Prince Labanoff, and other ancient families,—various foreign libraries, and many sources of private information, in the correspondence of the times, preserved among the archives of noble families, both in England and Scotland. She also waded through the quartos of the Bannatyne and Maitland, the Abbotsford and Spalding Clubs, and the published works of continental writers; every page of her work teeming with authorities and quotations.

She was born, in 1806, at the family residence, Reydon Hall, in Suffolk; and died in 1874. She was the third of five daughters, all of whom distinguished themselves by the pen, as, indeed, did their only brother, Major Strickland, author of "Twenty-seven years in Canada West." The eldest sister, Elizabeth—as I have already said—helped Agnes largely in her historical works. Jane, the second, began, when very young, to write in the annuals and religious magazines, and was author of "Rome, Regal and Republican." The fourth sister, Catharine Parr, is better known as Mrs. Traill, author of "The Backwoods of America," and "A Guide to Female Emigrants"; and the fifth daughter, Susannah, Mrs. Moodie, is well-known by her popular work, "Roughing it in the Bush," and is author of two novels, "Flora Lindsay," and "Mark Huddlestone."

At the age of twelve, Agnes Strickland was writing a lengthy rhymed chronicle on the Wars of the Roses; and, at the age of fifteen she had published her first book—a collection of historical poems, called "Worcester Field; or The Cavalier," which was highly eulogised by the poet, Thomas Campbell. She then contributed to various magazines; and, at the age of twenty-one, issued another volume of verse, called "The Seven Ages of Woman." Other volumes followed, both in prose and verse; but, it was not until the year 1840, that the first volume of her "Queens of England" was published. From that day, till her death, her labours were chiefly in the study of English and Scottish History, of which her Life of Mary, Queen of Scots, is one of her most conspicuous achievements.

Her friendship was very pleasant to me, and may fitly be recorded here, as my introduction to her was through the medium of Fotheringhay and Mary, Queen of Scots.

PORTRAITS OF MARY, QUEEN OF SCOTS.

If many parts of the earlier life of Mary, Queen of Scots, present a puzzled problem to the historian, and, as Sir Walter Scott says, "an unexplained riddle to posterity," her numerous portraits present a like bewilderment to those who would wish to see what this acknowledged peerless queen of beauty was like. The portraits of Mary Stuart are very numerous, and not only greatly vary, but, in some cases, are anything but pleasing.

I think that to Sir Walter Scott must be given the palm of those writers who have attempted a description of her face and form. In the 21st chapter of his novel, "The Abbot," he introduces her to the reader, as a prisoner at Lochleven Castle, in the following glowing terms:—

"Her face, her form, have been so deeply impressed upon the imagination, that, even at the distance of nearly three centuries, it is unnecessary to remind the most ignorant and uninformed reader of the striking traits which characterize that remarkable countenance, which seems at once to combine our ideas of the majestic, pleasing and the brilliant, leaving us to doubt whether they express most happily the queen, the beauty, or the accomplished woman. Who is there, that, at the very mention of Mary Stuart's name, has not her countenance before him, familiar as that of the mistress of his youth, or the favourite daughter of his advanced age? Even those who feel themselves compelled to believe all, or much, of what her enemies laid to her charge, cannot think without a sigh upon a countenance expressive of anything rather than the foul crimes with which she was charged when living, and which still continue to shade, if not to blacken, her memory. That brow, so truly open and regal,—those eyebrows, so regularly graceful, which yet were saved from the charge of regular insipidity by the beautiful effect of the hazel eyes which they overarched, and which seem to utter a thousand histories,—the nose, with all its Grecian precision of outline, —the mouth, so well-proportioned, so sweetly formed, as if designed to speak nothing but what was delightful to hear,—the dimpled chin,—the stately swan-like neck—form a countenance, the like of which we know not to have existed in any other character moving in that class of life, where the actresses as well as the actors command general and undivided attention.

"It is in vain to say that the portraits which exist of this most remarkable woman are not like each other; for, amidst their discrepancy, each possesses general features which the eye at once acknowledges as peculiar to the vision which our imagination has raised while we read her history for the first time, and which has been impressed upon it by the numerous prints and pictures which we have seen. Indeed, we cannot look on the worst of them, however deficient in point of execution, without saying that it is meant for Queen Mary; and no small instance is it of the power of beauty, that her charms should have remained the subject not merely of admiration, but of warm and chivalrous interest, after such a length of time. We know that by far the most acute of those who, in latter days, have adopted the unfavourable view of Mary's character, longed, like the executioner before his dreadful task was performed, to kiss the fair hand of her on whom he was about to perform so horrible a duty."

Chalmers, in hopeless perplexity, made his draughtsman produce a composite portrait of Mary, Queen of Scots, taking the hair from one picture, the nose from another, the eyes from another, and so on. It has been observed, that the portraits bearing Mary's name, may be assigned to four divisions:—first, those of pure imagination; secondly, the portraits painted in France; thirdly, the portrait painted in Sheffield, in 1578, by P. Oudry, of which there are numerous duplicates, and a copy of which was painted, by Mytens, for

James I; and, fourthly, the pictures painted after the execution, of which, three at least are in existence, the original being that given by Elizabeth Curle to Blair's College, and already described in these pages. All the pictures of Mary, possessing any claim to authenticity may be traced to one of these three sources; and, in all the pictures, the same features may be seen. As a matter of course, where some artists succeeded, others failed; and some of the picture-painters had an intense incapacity to do justice to their lovely sitter. But, the same characteristics are to be found in the majority of the portraits; while some that are dubbed as portraits of the Queen of Scots, are, no doubt, representations of some other lady of that period.

As an instance of this, I may mention the following fact:—Mr. Gordon, of Sloane Street, being in Florence, watched a clever young French artist, M. Averani, copying the Venus Vesita, of Titian, in the Pitti Palace, said to be the only miniature painted by that great man. It was painted on a gold ground, and had a good deal of the character of Mary Stuart. Mr. Gordon purchased it for six sequins, and brought it to England. Afterwards, when Mr. Gordon sold his Sloane Street Collection, previous to settling in Scotland, the copy of the Titian, was bought for fifty-five guineas. Soon after, the purchaser exhibited it at 14, Pall Mall, charging half-a-crown admission, as "an original portrait of Mary, Queen of Scotland, the undoubted work of Titian, value one thousand guineas." The exhibitor cleared between three and four hundred pounds by the transaction, besides selling the miniature to a nobleman for nearly eight hundred pounds.

Some of the portraits of Mary, Queen of Scots, have already been mentioned in these pages. A collection of her portraits was exhibited at Edinburgh, July, 1856, in connection with the meeting of the Archœological Institute of Great Britain and Ireland; another collection, including the Blairs College picture, was afterwards exhibited at Aberdeen; and another collection at the National Portrait Exhibition, at South Kensington, in May, 1866. In addition to the copy of the Blairs College portrait, Miss Agnes Strickland gives steel engravings of the portrait of Mary when Queen-Dauphiness, from the original presented by herself to the Earl of Cassillis—of Mary, in her 25th year, from the picture presented by herself to Sir Henry Curwen, of Workington Hall, Cumberland—and of Mary, in her widow's weeds, from the picture presented by herself to her deliverer, Willie Douglas, and now in the collection of the Earl of Morton, at Dalmahoy.

The portrait of Mary, Queen of Scots—of which a photograph is given in this volume—is here published for the first time. It is a highly finished miniature, on copper, and was given to me by Mr. Cecil, as a friendly acknowledgment for the additions that I made to his Mary Stuart collection, now in the possession of the nation, and spoken of in a previous page. Mr. Cecil purchased the picture in France when he was making his collection, and it was believed by himself and other experts to be a contemporary portrait. He gave it to me in the year 1853, and it has been in my possession ever since. Many who have seen it hanging in my drawing-room, have been well qualified to give an opinion as to its merits and age; and they have pronounced it to be, what Mr. Cecil believed it to be, a contemporary portrait.

The following Sonnet on "Fotheringhay: 1885," has been specially written for this volume:—

A lofty mound, with aged thorns encrowned,
With grass o'ergrown, and decked with golden flowers;
A hoary fragment of the ruined towers,
On the green slope, a flaggy moat around;
Sole, sad, memorials of the once renowned,
And stately castle, form a quiet scene;
While floweth idly by the placid Nene,
Appropriate emblem of the peace profound.
Here Memory comes, and musing o'er the past,
Sees through the vista of three hundred years,
Scots' hopeless Queen, captive, with scarce a friend,
Her fate foreboding, gray too soon through tears:—
Those bitter bonds of suffering loosed at last,
By that fell, cruel, stroke, that tragic end.

—*N. E. Dixon.*

Notes.

NOTES.

PAGE 95.—One of the Peers who was absent from the Trial, though he was present at the Execution, was the Earl of Shrewsbury, who was excused from attending on account of indisposition. He would appear to have been on his way to Fotheringhay; for, he lay at Stilton, probably, at the "Bell," on the Great North Road, where he was visited by Lord Burghley, who gave him an account of the Trial.

PAGE 103.—The letter written by Lord Burghley to Secretary Davison was as follows:

"Fotheringhay, October 15, 1586.

Mr. Secretary,—Yesternight, upon receipt of your letter dated on Thursday, I writ what was thought to be this day's work. This Queen of the Castle was content to appear again afore us in public to be heard, but in truth, not to be heard for her defence, for she could say nothing but negatively, 'that the points of the letters that concerned the practise against the queen's majesty's person, were never written by her, nor of her knowledge; the rest for invasion, for escaping by force, she said she would neither deny nor affirm.' But, her intention was, by long artificial speeches, to move pity, to lay all the blame upon the queen's majesty, or rather upon the council, that all the troubles past did ensue, avowing her reasonable offers and our refusals; and in these her speeches, I did so encounter her with reasons out of my knowledge and experience, as she had not that advantage she looked for; as I am sure the auditory did find her case not pitiable, her allegations untrue, by which means great debate fell yesternight very long, and this day renewed, with great stomaching.

And we find all persons here in the commission fully satisfied, as by her majesty's order, judgement will be given at our next meeting, but the record will not be provided in five or six days, and that was one cause why, if we should have proceeded to judgement, we should have tarried five or six days more; and surely the country could not bear it, by the waste of bread specially, our company being there, and within six miles, above 2000 horsemen, but by reason of her majesty's letter, we of her council, that is, the Lord Chancellor, Mr. Rich, Mr. Secretary and myself only, did procure this prorogation, for the other two causes.

And so, knowing that by my Lord of Cumberland, her majesty shall, sooner than this letter can come, understand the course of the proceeding, I will end.

Your assured loving friend,

W. BURGHLEY."

PAGE 108.—The letter written by the Queen of Scots to Queen Elizabeth was in French. The following is a full translation:

"Fotheringhay, December 19th, 1586.

Madame,—Having, with difficulty, obtained leave from those to whom you have committed me, to open to you all I have on my heart, as much for exonerating myself from any ill-will, or desire of committing cruelty, or any act of enmity against those with whom I am connected in blood; as also, kindly to communicate to you what I thought would serve you, as much for your weal and preservation, as for the maintenance of the peace and repose of this isle, which can only be injured if you reject my advice. You will credit, or disbelieve my discourse, as seems best to you.

I am resolved to strengthen myself in Christ Jesus alone, who, to those invoking Him with a true heart, never fails in His justice and consolation, especially to those who are bereft of all human aid; such are under His holy protection; to Him be the glory! He has equalled my expectation, having given me heart and strength, *in spe contra spem*, to endure the unjust calumnies, accusations and condemnations (of those who have no such jurisdiction over me), with a constant resolution to suffer death, for upholding the obedience and authority of the apostolical Roman Catholic Church.

Now since I have been on your part informed of the sentence of your last meeting of Parliament, Lord Buckhurst and Beale having admonished me to prepare for the end of my long and weary pilgrimage, I beg to return you thanks on my part for these happy tidings, and to entreat you to vouchsafe to me certain points for the discharge of my conscience. But since Sir A. Paulet has informed me (though falsely) that you had indulged me by having restored to me my almoner and the money that they had taken from me, and that the remainder would follow; for all this I would willingly return you thanks, and supplicate still further as a last request, which I have thought for many reasons I ought to ask of you alone, that you will accord this ultimate grace, for which I should not like to be indebted to any other, since I have no hope of finding aught but cruelty, from the puritans, who are at this time, God knows wherefore, the first in authority and the most bitter against me.

I will accuse no one; may I pardon, with a sincere heart, every one, even as I desire every one may grant forgiveness to me, God the first. But I know that you, more than any one, ought to feel at heart the honoùr or dishonour of your own blood, and that, moreover, of a queen and the daughter of a king.

Then, madame, for the sake of that Jesus to whose name all powers bow, I require you to ordain, that when my enemies have slaked their black thirst for my innocent blood, you will permit my poor desolated servants altogether to carry away my corpse, to bury it in holy ground, with the other Queens of France, my predecessors, especially near the late Queen, my mother; having this in recollection, that, in Scotland, the bodies of the Kings, my predecessors, have been outraged, and the churches profaned and abolished; and that as I shall suffer in this country, I shall not be given place near the Kings your predecessors, who are mine as well as yours; for, according to our religion, we think much of being interred in holy earth. As they tell me that you will in nothing force my conscience nor my religion, and have even conceded me a priest, refuse me not this my last request, that you will permit free sepulchre to this body when the soul is separated, which when united could never obtain liberty to live in repose, such as you would procure for yourself—against which repose, before God I speak, I never aimed a blow; but God will let you see the truth of all after my death.

And, because I dread the tyranny of those to whose power you have abandoned me, I entreat you not to permit that execution be done on me without your own knowledge; not for fear of the torment, which I am most ready to suffer, but on account of the reports which will be raised concerning my death unsuspected, and without other witnesses than those who would inflict it, who, I am persuaded, would be of very different qualities from those parties whom I require (being my servants) to stay spectators and with witnesses of my end, in the faith of our Sacrament, of my Saviour, and in obedience to His Church. And, after all is over, that they together may carry away my poor corpse (as secretly as you please) and speedily withdraw, without taking with them any of my goods, except those which, in dying, I may leave to them, which are little enough for their long and good services.

One jewel that I received of you, I shall return to you with my last words, or sooner if you please.

Once more I supplicate you to permit me to send a jewel and a last adieu to my son, with my dying benediction, for of my blessing he has been deprived, since you sent me his refusal to enter into the treaty whence I was excluded by his wicked council; this last point I refer to your favourable consideration and conscience, as the others; but I ask them, in the name of Jesus Christ, and in respect of our consanguinity, and for the sake of King Henry VII, your grandfather and mine, and by the honour and dignity we both held, and of our sex in common, do I implore you to grant these requests.

As to the rest, I think you know, that, in your name, they have taken down my dais; but afterwards they owned to me that it was not by your commandment, but by the intimation of some of your privy council; I thank God that this wickedness came not from you, and that it serves rather to vent their malice than to afflict me, having made up my mind to die. It is on account of this, and some other things, that they debarred me from writing to you; and, after they had done all in their power to degrade me from my rank, they told me 'that I was but a mere dead woman, incapable of dignity.' God be praised for all!

I would wish that all my papers were brought to you without reserve, that, at last it may be manifest to you, that the sole care of your safety was not confined to those who are so prompt to persecute me; if you will accord this, my last request, I would wish that you would write for them, otherwise they do with them as they choose. And, moreover, I wish that to this, my last request, you will let me know your last reply.

To conclude, I pray God, the just Judge, of His mercy, that He will enlighten you with His Holy Spirit, and that He will give me His grace to die in the perfect charity I am disposed to do, and to pardon all those who have caused, or co-operated in, my death. Such will be my last prayer, to my end, which I esteem myself happy will precede the persecution which, I foresee, menaces this isle, where God is no longer seriously feared and revered, but vanity and worldy policy rule and govern all—yet, will I accuse no one, nor give way to presumption—yet, while abandoning this world and preparing myself for a better, I must remind you, that one day you will have to answer for your charge, and for all those whom you doom, and that I desire that my blood and my country may be remembered in that time. For why? From the first days of our capacity to comprehend our duties, we ought to bend our minds to make the things of this world yield to those of eternity.

From Fotheringhay this 19th December, 1586,

Your sister and cousin,

Prisoner wrongfully,

MARIE (ROYNE).*

PAGE 110.—Queen Elizabeth's conduct and language at this period are thus described by the French historian, F. A. Mignet (translation by A. R. Scoble, Vol. II, p. 344-8.) "Elizabeth did not yield to the solicitations of Burghley, Leicester and Walsingham, but she became thoughtful and gloomy. She neglected her usual amusements, indulged in solitude, and frequently muttered terrible words. She was heard to pronounce a Latin sentence, which served to indicate her anxiety:—"Aut fer aut feri; ne feriare feri."—"Strike, or be struck; if you would not be struck, strike." She would have been glad if anyone would have relieved her, by secret assassination, of the responsibility of a legal execution. She hinted to her ministers that they should put Mary to death, and spare her the cruel task of giving the order; and she reproached them with having promised largely when they took the famous oath of the Association, and yet doing nothing for her defence. But the responsibility which she hesitated to take upon herself, her ministers refused to incur. They knew her too well not to feel assured that she would disown them the very day after they had ministered to her passion; and that she would even punish them, so as to throw upon

* In the days of her prosperity she merely signed her name "Marie"; but, after her captivity, she was careful to add R. or Royne (for *Regina*), for the purpose of asserting that royalty, of which she declared she had been deprived by violence and hard restraint, at Lochleven. (See the Egerton Papers, and Miss Strickland's "Letters of Mary, Queen of Scots.")

them all the odium of an execution, of which she desired the advantage without the blame. They turned, therefore, a deaf ear to her hints, and the Queen was compelled to act directly herself.

On the 1st of February, Secretary Davison, for whom she had sent by Lord Admiral Howard, presented himself before her, at ten o'clock in the morning, with the warrant for Mary's execution, which had beer previously drawn up by the High Treasurer, Burghley. She took it into her hands, read it, asked for a pen, and signed it firmly, desiring Davison to cause the Lord Chancellor to affix to it the Seal of State. She recommended it to be kept as much as possible secret, and added, with an air of pleasantry, "Show it, nevertheless, to Walsingham: I fear the blow will kill him on the spot." She forbade a public execution, directing that it should take place in the great hall of Fotheringhay, and not in the court of the castle, and she dismissed Davison with an injunction that she was not again to be addressed on the subject, having done all that the law and reason could require of her.

Just as he was on the point of withdrawing, Elizabeth detained him, and complained of Amias Paulet and those who might have relieved her of this burden. She added, that she might still be freed of it, if he and Walsingham would write to Sir Amias to sound him on the subject. Whether from want of conscientiousness, or from excess of obedience, Davison did not reject this frightful proposal, but communicated it immediately to Walsingham, while he exhibited the Act signed by the Queen. That very day they wrote to Fotheringhay, and, in that age, when assassination was not disavowed by any sect, and was repugnant to no political party, two ministers of a powerful sovereign, dared, in her name, to instigate the keepers of a prisoner to put her to death clandestinely. Here is the insidious and abominable letter which they jointly addressed to Paulet and Drury ;—

"After our cordial greetings, we perceive, from some words lately spoken by her Majesty, that she remarks in you a want of diligence and zeal in not having discovered of yourselves (without other instigation) some mode of putting that Queen to death, considering the great danger to which her Majesty is exposed, so long as the said Queen is in life. Not to speak of the want of affection to her, her Majesty remarks further, that you do not consider your own safety, or rather the preservation of religion, of the public weal, and of the prosperity of your country, as reason and policy require you to do. Your conscience would be peaceful before God, and your reputation clear before the world, since you have taken the solemn oath of the Association, and since, moreover, the facts charged against that Queen have been already proved. Her Majesty, therefore, feels great displeasure at men who profess attachment to her, as you do, thus failing in their duty, and seeking to throw on her the weight of this affair, well knowing, as you do, her repugnance to the shedding of blood, particularly that of a person of her sex and of her rank, and so near a relative.

We perceive that these considerations trouble her Majesty greatly, who, we can assure you, has repeatedly declared that if she did not feel a greater concern for the dangers which her faithful subjects and her good servants run, than for those which threaten herself, she would never consent that this Queen's blood should be shed. We think it very necessary to inform you of these sentiments expressed not long since by her Majesty, and to submit them to your good judgment, and so we recommend you to the Almighty's protection."

This letter, which Davison begged Paulet to burn after having read it, arrived at Fotheringhay, on the second of February, towards evening. One hour afterwards, Paulet, who was a sombre fanatic, and a brutal gaoler, but not a dastardly murderer, replied to Walsingham in terms of deep concern and repressed indignation.

"Having received your letter of yesterday at five o'clock in the afternoon of this day, I could not fail to send you an answer with all possible despatch, as you direct. I send it to you in all the bitterness which my heart feels as being so unfortunate as to see the day when, by the injunctions of my most gracious Sovereign, I am required to commit an act which God and the laws forbid. My property, my place, and my life are at her Majesty's disposal, and I am ready to surrender them to-morrow, it such is her good pleasure, acknowledging that I hold them from her sole and gracious favour; I do not wish to enjoy them but with the good-will of her Highness. But God preserve me from making such a pitiable shipwreck of my conscience, or leaving so foul a stain on my posterity, as to shed blood without the authority of the law, and without a public Act. I hope her Majesty, with her accustomed clemency, will take my loyal answer in good part, as proceeding from one who never will be inferior to any Christian subject living in honour, love and obedience towards his Sovereign, and thus I commit you to the mercy of the Almighty. Your most assured poor friend,

A. POWLET.

From Fotheringhay, the 2nd of February, 1586-7.

P.S. Your letters coming in the plural number, seem to be meant to Sir Drue Drury as to myself, and yet because he is not named in them, neither the letters directed unto him, he forbeareth to make any particular answer, but subscribeth in heart to my opinion.

D. DRURY."*

Davison, in his narrative, says that when the Queen read the letter, "she fell into some terms of offence complaining of the dainty perjury of Sir Amyas, who, contrary to his oath of Association, would lay the whole burden of this death upon her. Then she took a turn or two on her gallery, whither Davison followed her, she renewing her former speech,

* This is not given by Mignet, but will be found in Miss Strickland's *Letters*, Vol. II, p. 232.

blaming the niceness of "that precise fellow, Paulet,"—for, so she called him now, instead of her former caressing epithets of "Amyas, my most careful and faithful servant." "For," she added, "in words he would do much, but in deeds perform nothing;" and concluded, "She would have it done without them;" naming one Wingfield, who, she assured Secretary Davison, "with some others, would undertake it"—namely, the private assassination of the Queen of Scots. She did not, however, find it so easy in England to obtain agents for private murder. "For," says Davison, "the next time I had access to her, she swore it was a shame to them all (her ministers and privy council) that it was not done."

PAGE 115.—THE WILL OF MARY, QUEEN OF SCOTS.

"In the name of the Father, of the Son, and of the Holy Ghost, I, Mary, by the Grace of God, Queen of Scotland and Dowager of France, being on the point of death, and not having any means of making my will, have myself committed these articles to writing, and I will and desire, that they have the same force, as if they were made in due form.

In the first place, I declare that I die in the Catholic, Apostolic, and Romish faith. First, I desire that a complete service be performed for my soul in the church of St. Denis, in France, and another in St. Peter's, at Rheims, where all my servants are to attend, in such manner as they may be ordered to do by those to whom I have given directions, and who are named therein.

Further, that an annual obit be founded for prayers for my soul, in perpetuity, in such place, and after such manner, as shall be deemed most convenient.

To furnish funds for this, I will that my houses at Fountainebleau be sold, hoping that the King will render me assistance, as I have requested him to do in my memorandum.

I will that my estate of Trespagny be kept by my cousin De Guise, for one of his daughters, if she should come to be married. In these quarters, I relinquish half of the arrears due to me, or a part, on condition that the other be paid, in order to be expended, by my executors, in perpetual alms.

To carry this into effect the better, the documents shall be looked out, and delivered according to the assignment for accomplishing this.

I will also that the money which may arise from my lawsuit with Secondat be distributed as follows :

First, in the discharge of my debts and orders hereafter mentioned, and which are not yet paid : in the first place, the two thousand crowns to Curle, which I desire to be paid without any hesitation, they being a marriage portion, upon which neither Nau nor any other person has any claim, whatever obligation he may hold, inasmuch as it is only fictitious, and the money is mine, and not borrowed, which since I did but show him, and afterwards withdrew it, and it was taken from me with the rest at Chartley ; the which I give him, provided he can recover it, agreeably to my promise, in payment of the four thousand francs promised at my death, one thousand is a marriage portion for an own sister, and he having asked me for the rest for his expenses in prison. As to the payment of a similar sum to Nau, it is not obligatory, and therefore it has always been my intention that it should be paid last, and then only in case he should make it appear that he has not acted contrary to the condition on which I gave it him, and to which my servants were witnesses.

As regards the twelve hundred crowns, which he has placed to my account, as having been borrowed by him for my use, six hundred of Beauregard, three hundred from Gervais, and the remainder from I know not whom, he must repay them out of his own money, and I must be quit, and my order annulled, as I have not received any part of it, consequently it must be still in his possession, unless he has paid it away. Be this as it may, it is necessary that this sum should revert to me,

I having received nothing; and, in case it has not been paid away, I must have recourse to his property. I further direct, that Pasquier shall account for the moneys that he has expended and received by order of Nau, from the hands of the servants of Monsieur de Chasteauneuf, the French ambassador.

Further, I will that my accounts be audited, and my treasurer paid.

Further, that the wages and sums due to my household, as well for the last as for the present year, be paid them before all other things, both wages and pensions, excepting the pensions of Nau and Curle, until it be ascertained what there is remaining, or whether they have merited any pensioning from me, unless the wife of Curle be in necessity, or be ill-treated on my account: the wages of Nau after the same manner.

I will that the two thousand four hundred francs which I have given to Jeanne Kennedy be paid to her in money, as it was stated in my first deed of gift, which done, the pension of Volly Douglas shall revert to me, which I give Fontenay for services and expenses, for which he has had no compensation.

I will that the four thousand francs of that banker's be applied for and repaid, I have forgotten his name, but the Bishop of Glascou will readily recollect it; and, if the first order be not honoured, I desire that another may be given on the first money from Secondat.

The ten thousand francs which the ambassador has received for me, I will that they be distributed among my servants who are now going away, viz.:

First, two thousand francs to my physician.
two thousand francs to Elizabeth Curle.
two thousand francs to Sebastien Paiges.
two thousand francs to Mairie Paiges, my god-daughter.
to Beauregard a thousand francs.
a thousand to Gervais.

Further, that, out of the rest of my revenue, with the remainder of Secondat's and all other casualties, I will that five thousand francs be given to the Foundling Hospital of Rheims.

To my scholars, two thousand francs.

To four mendicants, such sum as my executors may think fit, according to the means in their hands.

Five hundred francs to the hospitals.

To Martin, *escuyer de cuisine*, I give a thousand francs.

A thousand francs to Annibal, whom I recommend to my cousin De Guise, his godfather, to place in some situation, for his life, in his servica.

I leave five hundred francs to Nicolas, and five hundred francs for his daughters, when they marry.

I leave five hundred francs to Robert Hamilton, and beg my son to take him, and Monsieur de Glascou, or the Bishop of Rosse.

I leave to Didier his registership, subject to the approbation of the King.

I give five thousand francs to Jean Landon, and beg my cousin of Guise, or of Mayne, to take him into their service, and Messieurs de Glascou and de Rosse to see him provided for. I will that his father be paid his wages, and leave him five hundred francs.

I will that one thousand francs be paid to Gourgeon, for money and other things with which he supplied me in my necessity.

I will that if Bourgoin should perform the journey agreeably to the vow, which he made for me to Saint Nicolas, that fifteen hundred francs be paid to him for that purpose.

I leave, according to my slender means, six thousand francs to the Bishop of Glascou, and three thousand to him of Rosse.

And I leave the gift of casualties and the reserved seignorial rights to my godson, the son of Monsieur de Ruisseu.

I give three hundred francs to Laurenz.

Also three hundred francs to Suzanne.

And leave ten thousand francs among the four persons who have been my sureties, and to Varmy the solicitor.

I will that the money arising from the furniture, which I have ordered to be sold in London, shall go to defray the travelling expenses of my servants in France.

My coach I leave to carry my ladies, and the horses, which they can sell, or do what they like with.

There remains about three hundred crowns due to Bourgoing for the wages of past years, which I desire may be paid him.

I leave two thousand francs to Melville, my steward.

I appoint my cousin, the Duke of Guise, the principal executor of my will.

After him, the Archbishop of Glascou, the Bishop of Rosse, and Monsieur de Ruisseu, my chancellor.

I desire that De Préan may, without obstacle, hold his two prebends.

I recommend Marie Paiges, my god-daughter, to my cousin, Madame de Guise, and beg her to take her into her service, and my aunt de Saint Pierre to get Moubray some good situation, or retain her in her service, for the honour of God.

Done this day, 7th February, 1587.

MARY, Queen.

Memorandum of the last request which I make to the King.

To cause to be paid to me, all that is due to me, of my pensions, as also of money advanced by the late Queen, my mother, in Scotland, for the service of the King, my father-in-law, in those parts: that at least an annual obit may be founded for my soul, and that the alms and the little endowments promised by me may be carried into effect.

Further, that he may be pleased to grant me the benefit of my dowry for one year after my death, to recompense my servants.

Further, that he may be pleased to allow them their wages and pensions during their lives, as was done to the officers of Queen Alienor. Further, I entreat him to take my physician into his service, according to his promise to consider him as recommended.

Further, that my almoner may be replaced in his profession, and, for my sake, have some trifling benefice conferred upon him, so that he may pray to God for my soul during the rest of his life.

Further, that Didier, an old officer of my household, whom I have recompensed by a registership, may be permitted to enjoy it for his life, being already far advanced in years.

Written on the morning of my death, this Wednesday, 8th of February, 1587.

MARIE R."

These were the last lines written by Mary, Queen of Scots.

PAGE 129.—According to the narrative of Pierre le Pesant Sieur du Bois Guilbert, "she knelt upright sometime, expecting her head to be taken off with the stroke of a sword, as they do in France. But, the executioner and his servant, having waited some time, placed her head on the block. The executioner then gave her a stroke with an axe of the same shape of those which they cleave wood withal, without doing any further harm than wounding her skull, so awkward was he; then, redoubling a second and third stroke, he at last cut off her head." Mignet says—"She imagined that she would have been struck in the mode usual in France, in an upright posture, and with the sword. The two masters of the works, perceiving her mistake, informed her of it, and assisted her to lay her head on the block, which she did without ceasing to pray. There was a universal feeling of compassion at the sight of this lamentable misfortune, this heroic courage, and this admirable sweetness.

The executioner himself was moved, and aimed with an unsteady hand. The axe, instead of falling on the neck, struck the back of the head and wounded her; yet, she made no movement, nor uttered a complaint. It was only on repeating the blow, that the executioner struck off her head." (II. 367.)

PAGE 131.—The "R. W." is believed to be Richard Wigmore, secret agent of Lord Burghley.

PAGE 139.—"The two Earls did not leave to the executioner, according to custom, the golden cross around her neck, the chaplets suspended to her girdle, nor the clothes she wore at her death, lest those dear and venerated spoils should be redeemed by her servants and transformed into relics. They therefore burned them." (Mignet.)

PAGE 145.—"The body of the Queen of Scots, after removing the entrails, which were secretly buried, was embalmed but with little respect, wrapped up in wax-cloth, enclosed in a leaden coffin, and left aside until Elizabeth should fix the place where it was to be laid." (Mignet). "Her Majesty's body was embalmed carelessly, and put, with the head, into a lead coffin, and that into another of wood, and they left it in the said great chamber until the first day of the month of August, without anybody being allowed to approach it all that time; the English perceiving that some of her people went to see it through the key-hole and pray to God, caused it to be stopped up." (Jebb.) The Mr. Blackwood who is mentioned on page 160, writes concerning this circumstance—"The corpes was carryed into a chamber next adjoining, fearinge the saide maides should come to do any charitable good office. It did increase greatly their desire so to do after they did see their mistress' corpes thorowe a little hole of the chamber wall. which was covered with cloath, but the wofull corpes was keepte a longe time in this chamber till it began to corrupt and smell strongly, so that in the end they were constrained to salt it, and to embalm lightly to save charges, and after to wrap it up in a cake of leade, keeping it seven months there before it was put into prophane earth in the church of Peterborough. It is very true that this church is dedicated under the name of Monsieur Saint Peter, and Queen Catherine of Spain was interred therein after the Catholique fashion, but it is now prophaned like all the churches of Englande."

PAGE 147.—A reason for the tardy state funeral of the murdered Queen of Scots is given by the Rev. G. Ayliffe Poole, in his *Diocesan History of Peterborough* :—"Her body was kept seven months unburied, probably, in hopes that her son, James, King of Scotland, would relieve Elizabeth of the cost of her obsequies." (p. 148.)

PAGE 156.—The tombs of Mary, Queen of Scots and Katharine of Arragon, in Peterborough Cathedral, with all their adornments and surroundings, were utterly destroyed by the Puritans, in their desecration of the building. When it was represented to King Henry VIII, that no worthy monument had been erected over the grave of his first wife, he replied that "she should have such a monument as no other wife ever had!" and he ordered that the Abbey Church should be the Cathedral of a new See. Which was a very cheap method for obtaining a royal memorial.

King James paid £3,500 for the monuments in Westminster Abbey to his mother, to Queen Elizabeth, and his two daughters, Mary and Sophia. The following description of the monument to Mary, Queen of Scots, is given by Brayley, (*Londiniana*, Vol. IV., p. 6.) "This monument, which stands in the south aisle, is an elaborate and costly architectural pile; like that of Queen Elizabeth in the north aisle, it is principally a composition from the Corinthian order, and of similar design: but its dimensions and elevation are much greater, the armorial crests which surmount the upper entablature reaching almost to the vaulting. It is constructed of different coloured marbles.

The basement is raised on a two-fold step or plinth, and has four projecting pedestals on each side near the ends: on these stand eight columns, supporting the entablature and canopy, beneath which, upon a sarcophagus, ornamented with lions' heads, is a recumbent statue of the Queen, very finely executed. Her head reposes on two embroidered cushions; and her hands are raised in prayer, but several of her fingers have been broken off. She wears a close coif, with a narrow edging, and a laced ruff and a tucker, both plaited. Her features are small, but peculiarly sweet and delicate. Her mantle, which is lined with ermine and fastened over the breast with a jewelled broach, is folded gracefully over her knees and legs. The borders of her stomacher are wrought with chain-work; and her vest has a row of small buttons down the middle, with knots on each side. Her shoes are high-heeled, and round at the toes; at her feet is the Scottish lion sitting, crowned, supporting the emblems of sovereignty.

The columns which sustain this canopy are fancifully diversified as to materials: the shafts of four of them being of black marble, and their bases and capitals of white marble, and the shafts, bases, &c., of four others, directly the reverse. Beneath the lower entablatures are circles surrounded by small cherubs, and upon them, over the cornice, are shields of arms and small obelisks. The underpart of the semicircular canopy is divided into several ranges of small pannelling thickly ornamented with roses and thistles, in complete relief. In the spandrils at the sides are angels, draped, holding chaplets; on the summit are large shields, with the royal arms and supporters of Scotland; and at the angles are four unicorns, now broken and somewhat displaced, supporting smaller shields charged with badges. The inscriptions, which are in Latin, include four verses of ten lines each, and record the unfortunate Queen's royal descent and relations, the extraordinary endowments, both of body and mind, the troubles of her life, her constancy in religion, and her resolution in death."

PAGE 161.—The device of the royal crown and lion with fleur-de-lys, that is placed on the cover of this volume, I have copied from the upper part of "The Helmet and Escutcheon" placed over the grave of Mary, Queen of Scots, in Peterborough Cathedral, at the time of her state funeral, in 1587, and remaining pendant over the grave in 1641, when the spot was visited by Dugdale, who made the drawing from which this device is taken.

Index.

SIMILAR TOPOGRAPHICAL AND HISTORICAL BOOKS BY

CUTHBERT BEDE,

Author of "Verdant Green," (J. Blackwood, 3s. 6d.) "Adventures of little Mr. Bouncer," (J. Blackwood, 2s. 6d.) "Photographic Pleasures," (T. Maclean, 7s. 6d.) "Nearer and Dearer," (Bentley, 3s.) "Curate of Cranston," (Saunders, Otley and Co., 10s. 6d.) "Happy Hours," (J. Blackwood, 3s. 6d.) "The Rooks' Garden," (S. Low and Co., 8s.) "Tales of College Life," (Clarke, 1s.) "Wit, Humour, and Satire," (J. Blackwood, 3s. 6d.) "Mattins and Muttons," (S. Low and Co., 16s.) "Fairy Fables," (Bentley, 5s.) "Love's Provocations," (Ward and Lock, 1s.)

"GLENCREGGAN: or a Highland Home in Cantire." With three maps, eight chromolithographs, and sixty-one woodcuts, from the Author's drawings. 2 vols., price 24s. (Longman and Co.)

"A TOUR IN TARTAN-LAND." 1 vol., price 10s. 6d. (Bentley.)

"THE WHITE WIFE, and other West-Highland Stories," with illustrations by the Author. 1 vol., price 6s. (Sampson, Low, and Co.)

"VISITORS' GUIDE to Roslin and Hawthornden." With photographs (various prices).

Also numerous papers on topographical and historical matters in "The Gentleman's Magazine," "Leisure Hour," "Illustrated London News," "The Graphic," "The Queen," "Once a Week," "Belgravia," "Churchman's Illustrated

Magazine," "London Society," "Notes and Queries," "Old Lincolnshire," "Northamptonshire Notes and Queries," "London Review," &c.

NOTICES OF THE PRESS ON SCOTTISH BOOKS.

"An original work and one of considerable research. It has a decided archæological value. The gentleman—and he is a good scholar—who writes under the pseudonym "Cuthbert Bede," has made a genuine contribution to literature."—*The Saturday Review.*

"Among the best of the minor works of the season."—*The Times.*

"Has a value of a solid kind."—*The London Review.*

"A thoughtful man will place the volume on his shelves side by side with "The Book of the Dean of Lismore."—*The Guardian.*

"Really an acceptable book. The illustrations are excellent."—*The Athenæum.*

"Shews intelligence and care. The description of scenery is a little after the manner of Mr. Ruskin."—*Saturday Review.*

"Two of the freshest volumes we have seen for many a day."—*The Field.*

"The book, although exclusively about a home locality, is, for rich varied interest, equal to any volumes of foreign travel that have been recently issued."—*The Witness.*

"Pleasant, readable, instructive."—*The Globe.*

"To say that it is readable, is the least that can be said in its favour."—*Argyllshire Herald.*

"Full of valuable information, sparkling with wit and humour, rich in variety and interest."—*Caledonian Mercury.*

"The best account we have yet seen. As a guide-book it is invaluable."—*John Bull.*

"The illustrations and maps add greatly to its value."—*Daily News.*

"The best handbook which the traveller can provide himself with."—*The Spectator.*

"Cannot be too strongly commended, or too highly admired."—*Edinburgh Weekly Herald.*

"The illustrations are very clever."—*The Scotsman.*

"Containing a very considerable amount of lore, both historical and archæological, which entitle the work to rank in quite another class than a mere account of a tour."—*Dublin Evening Mail.*

"The book is one of the pleasantest that you can lay hands on."—*The Scottish Press.*

"Will be extensively popular."—*Atlas.*

"A wonderfully lightsome and readable book."—*Glasgow Daily Herald.*

"A very pleasant book, desultory yet not losing its way, digressive yet systematic in its wanderings."—*Morning Post.*

"A very readable book. We can commend it for the fulness and general accuracy of its facts."—*Edinburgh Evening Courant.*

"Cuthbert Bede is an amusing and instructive companion."—*Notes and Queries.*

"Worth a host of so-called Guide-books."—*Midland Free Press.*

"Cuthbert Bede is now known to the antiquarian world as an authority upon the subject of northern antiquities."—*The Standard.*

"The author possesses great powers of observation, joined to descriptive powers of no ordinary kind."—*Glasgow Examiner.*

"We may safely recommend the volume as a most useful and pleasant hand-book."—*Aris's Birmingham Gazette.*

"The style is clear, lively, and entertaining. The historical and topographical portions of the work are wonderfully correct, and worked out with considerable labour and skill."—*Glasgow Citizen.*

"The historical and topographical objects are related and depicted in a clear, cheerful, and happy manner."—*Perthshire Advertiser.*

"He has caught a degree of inspiration from the *genius loci*, which is reflected most delightfully in his pleasant pages."—*Worcester Herald.*

OUNDLE:

ALFRED KING, PRINTER.

1886.

14

Ingram Content Group UK Ltd.
Milton Keynes UK
UKHW020347300523
422541UK00005B/138

9 781017 792690